Dynamics of Public Relations and Journalism

Dynamics of Public Relations and Journalism

A practical guide for media studies

—–– **Third Edition** —–

Editor
Annette Clear
MA Communication

Contributors
Veena Parboo Rawjee
DPhil (Media and Communication)

Lydie Terblanche
PhD Media Studies

Zwakele Baldwin Ngubane

Nisha Ramlutchman

JUTA

First Edition 1997
Second Edition 2001
Third Edition 2011

First Floor, Sunclare Building
21 Dreyer Street
Claremont, 7708

© 2011 Juta and Company Ltd

ISBN 978-0-70217-813-9

Publisher: Rainhardt Genis
Project manager: Corina Pelser
Editor: Wendy Priilaid
Proofreader: Jenni Middleton Horn
Typesetter: Unwembi
Cover designer: Marius Roux
Printed and bound by Academic Press, Parow Industria, Cape Town, RSA

Picture credits:
Figure 14.2, p 175: Courtesy of Z PR Communication Consultants
Figure 16.2A, p 201: Courtesy of Marilette Henning
Figure 16.2B, p 201: Courtesy of Z PR Communication Consultants

CONTENTS

Preface

Unravelling the complex worlds of public relations and journalism in a single publication is not easy. However, when the dynamics of these two unique occupations are established, their interaction is easily apparent.

This book follows a unique approach, illustrating how public relations and journalism interact in the field of Media Studies. The subject forms a major part of the National Diploma in Public Relations Management at South African Universities of Technology (UoTs). To relate the subject more closely to the diploma course, this work shifts the strong emphasis currently placed on journalistic skills to public relations and media handling. It also focuses on the journalistic skills that the public relations practitioner needs to complete technical tasks effectively.

The material, including various practical examples and exercises, is derived from a South African perspective. This gives the user meaningful insights into the relationship between public relations and journalism in this country. Public relations practitioners are able to familiarise themselves with the complexities of journalism, and journalists gain an understanding of the public relations practitioner's media-handling role.

The book is divided into three distinct parts. Part 1 examines the basics of public relations and journalism and their interaction. It also establishes what news is and determines where it is to be found. Part 2, which investigates the South African mass-communication media, focuses on the print and electronic media. The structures and functions of the editorial newsrooms of the different media are discussed. The reader is shown how the public relations practitioner and the journalist combine their expertise to publish news. Part 2 further introduces new media, including social media and the role that the electronic media plays in both professions. Part 3 is a practical, step-by-step guide to the journalistic skills that public relations practitioners need, and focuses on interviewing, photography, writing, editing and design and page layout.

The authors of this practical manual have relied on their own extensive experience in public relations and journalism, making little use of existing publications. They address the many problems public relations students under their supervision experience in the subject of Media Studies.

With the help of this text, public relations students, practitioners, journalists and managers in every sector of the South African economy, should gain a better understanding of the unique, mutually beneficial relationship enjoyed by those in public relations and journalism.

Written in an interactive style, the book encourages the reader to take part in a quest to understand the attributes shared by the two disciplines and to appreciate their importance to each other.

Acknowledgements

Although we realised that students needed a detailed book giving a clear exposition of the interaction between public relations and journalism, it was only after a great deal of encouragement that we decided to put our thoughts and experience into a single, comprehensive publication, closing the gap in the available literature.

Sadly, my co-author, Linda Weideman, passed away in 2008, but her legacy lives on in this third edition, as we continue to build on the cornerstones she laid down with so much enthusiasm and an endless well of knowledge.

This book could not have been written without the assistance and support we received from several people.

We thank the staff of the South African Broadcasting Corporation for opening the complex world of the electronic media to the public relations practitioner. We are also grateful to spokespersons from various print media for their invaluable input.

On the academic side, we are indebted to Professor Arrie de Beer of the University of Potchefstroom who believed the book would contribute to a greater understanding and appreciation of both professions. His time and effort during the preparatory stages of the first edition are greatly appreciated.

To our colleague and friend, Ingrid van Jaarsveld, who unselfishly shared her public relations and journalistic skills with us and gave her impressions of and ideas on each chapter, thank you!

Linda's passing opened an opportunity for fellow educators to step in and contribute their valuable expertise and experience to the uniqueness of this book. As editor, I am therefore very grateful to my new co-contributors, Lydie Terblanche, Veena Parboo Rawjee and her team, Nisha Ramlutchman and Zwakele Baldwin Ngubane, for acknowledging the value that this book brings to students of Media Studies. Their enthusiasm, support and contribution to this new edition most certainly opens up the synergy between public relations and journalism even more.

Last but not least, we thank all Juta's editing and technical staff for their invaluable assistance in publishing the first, second and now the third edition.

Annette Clear
Editor
2010

PUBLIC RELATIONS AND JOURNALISM — AN INTRODUCTION

Public relations and journalism are two distinct disciplines, each having its own functions and objectives. However, the relationship between public relations and journalism is and always has been a complex and necessary symbiotic liaison of mutual dependence.

The relationship between these two communication professions is under constant pressure. The increasing professionalism of the management of news on the side of public relations and the explosive growth in media supply that resulted in increased competition between journalists and an intense contest for the news are two factors creating pressure.

The most important function they share is the conveying of newsworthy information. Public relations practitioners execute the publicity function by providing information to the media and journalists seek out the public relations practitioner for news material. Both public relations practitioners and journalists have to understand what makes news and what is important to the defined audience. The main differences between them are the manner in which they convey this information and their reasons for doing so. This can be easily understood when comparing the different purposes and roles of each profession.

Misconceptions by public relations students of the roles of professionals in these two fields lead to practical misunderstandings. These adversely affect the relationship enjoyed by public relations practitioners and journalists. Public relations practitioners dealing with the media must understand the opportunities and limitations to engaging in the journalistic process of story creation. Public relations facilitates media coverage and is therefore a necessary component of the media work process.

One of the public relations practitioner's main tasks is to deal with the mass communication media to carry a specific message, to promote an image or an idea, to defend a cause or just carry influence. Many practitioners fail to achieve their objective because they do not have sufficient experience and knowledge of, firstly, what the media consider newsworthy; secondly, preparing material in a way acceptable to the media; and thirdly, dealing with journalists.

Public relations practitioners and consultants are often called to task by management for not achieving sufficient media publicity. Usually, this failure can be pinned on lacking an awareness of the electronic and print media's primary need, to publish or broadcast information that can be construed as NEWS.

Identifying newsworthy information and presenting it appropriately to the media is essential. If publicity is to be gained, each news medium has to be approached in its preferred manner. The skills required to do this can also be applied when advising management of the complexity of the mass-communication media. If management is sympathetic, it will put less pressure on public relations practitioners to 'deliver'.

To a large extent, journalists depend on public relations practitioners for material to fill their publications and news slots. The gathering of newsworthy information is essential to a mass-communication medium's survival. Journalists report and cover events every day for news outlets and mass media. The more successful the media are in gathering and conveying newsworthy information, the higher their circulation and viewer figures will be. As it is the task of public relations practitioners to handle the media and to act as a link between them and management, they play a major role in giving journalists access to newsworthy information.

There is often a conception among journalists from the mass-communication media that public relations practitioners only cover up and do not supply the real hard facts. Journalists are sometimes sceptical about information received by the public relations department on controversial issues. Public relations practitioners should always remember that the media want to cover the full story and will, in most cases, consult other sources as well. They should take care to provide factual information and be credible at all times. At the same time, journalists should trust public relations practitioners regardless of how unpopular or politically incorrect the message is.

Both professions must understand that the relationship is more symbiotic than conflictual on condition that each profession does not try to step onto the other's turf.

Part 1 serves as an introduction to the fields of public relations and journalism. We look briefly at the purpose, role and responsibility of each profession. We then establish how public relations and journalism are interrelated and can be combined into an area of study called 'Media Studies'. In the third chapter we deal with the important subject of news and discuss how the public relations practitioner can identify and gather newsworthy information that will be acceptable to the media. The fourth chapter deals with ethics in public relations and journalism.

What are public relations and journalism?

Objectives

After you have studied this chapter, you should be able to:

▶ define public relations (PR) and journalism;
▶ discuss the purpose and role of public relations in an organisation; and
▶ discuss the purpose and role of the journalist employed by the *mass communication media*.

Introduction

This chapter gives an introductory overview of public relations and journalism. It will enable you to differentiate between public relations and journalism and to identify their purpose and roles.

This chapter aims to illustrate how the subject 'Media Studies' embraces public relations and journalism and to help develop cross-industry editorial and production skills. For public relations purposes, Media Studies is two-sided. On the one hand, public relations practitioners need a working knowledge of the available mass communication media and the skills to deal with their journalists. On the other hand, they need specific journalistic skills including interviewing, article writing, photography, page layout, etc to produce internal and external *house publications*.

Mass communication media: technical channels used to convey messages to a large, diverse audience (general public), eg radio, television, newspapers, magazines, etc.

House publication: a publication reporting events in an organisation – aimed at employees (internal) and groups outside the organisation (external)

The following diagram illustrates the place of public relations and journalism in Media Studies.

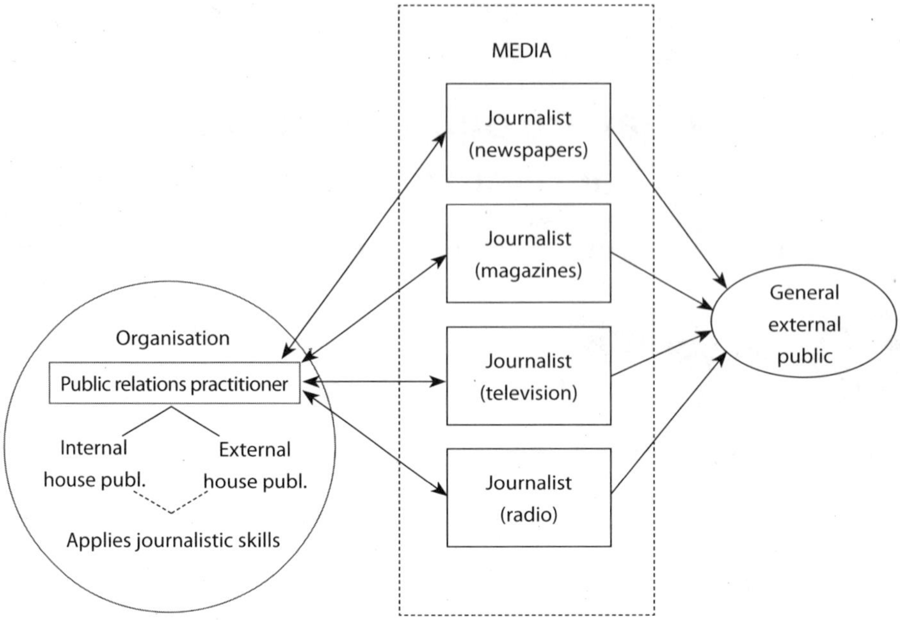

Figure 1.1 The link between public relations, journalists and Media Studies

Public relations practitioners deal with journalists from various media who publish or broadcast newsworthy information for, or to, the general public. To deal effectively with each journalist, public relations practitioners need to know how each medium functions. (This is dealt with in Media Studies.) Furthermore, public relations practitioners are responsible for internal and external house publications. They need to apply skills corresponding to those of journalists when fulfilling this task. (Journalistic skills are also dealt with in Media Studies).

 # A Public relations

Definition of public relations

 **Exercise**

Describe, in your own words, the term 'public relations'

Compare your description to the definition given below.

'Public relations is the management, through communication, of perceptions and strategic relationships between an organisation and its internal and external stakeholders' – **Defined by the Public Relations Institute of Southern Africa**

Although several other definitions are often used, this definition describes the concept of public relations most appropriately, and also makes it clear that effective communication has to take place. Communication is the backbone of public relations. Public relations practitioners must familiarise themselves with the many communication forms and techniques available for establishing effective communication with their organisation's *target groups*.

Target groups: specific, identified groups that are important to the organisation, eg schools, the local community, the general public

Public relations in organisations

Public relations practitioners are appointed by an organisation for an important task, namely to build the image of the company and to improve communication. In other words, when disseminating information, they are involved in and concerned about their organisation only.

Today, public relations is regarded as one of the most important components of any organisation. More and more, organisations are realising its great value. However, many managers still underestimate the role and functions of public relations, which is why public relations practitioners often have to fight for their profession to take its rightful place in their organisations. If they encounter such problems, they should educate management in the value and benefits of sound public relations.

Once management understands the place and role of public relations in the organisation, public relations practitioners will be able to function with management support. Because they often have to discuss and clarify aspects of policy and sensitive issues, they should have direct access to the head of the organisation.

Having said that, not all managers understand public relations, and it is also true that managements' perceptions that public relations practitioners are sometimes inadequately trained for their demanding profession and often lack necessary skills are, at times, well-founded. Public relations practitioners should not allow this perception to persist, and should ensure that they are qualified and competent in all aspects of public relations.

The purpose of public relations

What, in your view, is the purpose of public relations?

Public relations concerns itself with developing an organisation's image by creating effective, two-way communication channels between management and employees and between management and the organisation's external target groups.

What do the terms 'image building' and 'two-way communication channels' mean? In your own words, write down what you think these two concepts describe. Compare your answer to the discussion below.

Image building

To 'promote an organisation's image', the public relations practitioner must ensure that an organisation's policies, products and services are acceptable to the public and that the public is aware of them. Public relations creates an understanding of and goodwill towards the organisation, which leads to greater confidence in the organisation. What the public knows or thinks of the organisation determines whether it has a positive or a negative image.

Communication

Two-way communication implies sending a message, receiving feedback from its receiver and establishing a mutual understanding of the message. The sender can use various channels to send a message to the receiver. The channel of choice depends on who the receiver is. Public relations uses different channels for internal and external communication.

Internal communication

Internal communication is communication between management and employees. The public relations practitioner acts as a link between management and employees by channelling information to the employees. The newsletter is such a channel of communication. The newsletter's 'Letters to the Editor' column serves as a feedback conduit through which employees can raise issues with management. The public relations practitioner should always communicate with employees through appropriate internal communication channels and not through mass communication media directed at a large and diverse audience.

If public relations practitioners are to establish internal communication channels through newsletters or various other publications directed at employees, they will need good writing skills and a knowledge of photography, graphics, etc. They will have to oversee the layout and design of these publications with the help of desktop publishing programs and hardware. These functions include some of the journalistic skills the public relations practitioner should acquire.

External communication

Factors including the type of organisation and the organisation's objectives, will determine with whom the organisation communicates. The public relations practitioner conveys messages to specific people outside the organisation through, for example, an external house publication. The people targeted could include the immediate community, shareholders, opinion leaders and other organisations. The journalistic skills mentioned in the previous paragraph are also used in producing external house publications.

The public relations practitioner might want to bring an issue to the attention of the general public — which forms part of the external target group. To do this effectively, the public relations practitioner should use the media (newspapers, magazines, radio, television, etc) as communication channels. The media are probably the public relations practitioner's most important channels of external communication. Since public relations seeks positive publicity for the organisation, public relations practitioners often use the mass communication media to achieve their goals.

Because of the media's importance, public relations practitioners must know their structures, functions and activities. They must also know how to deal with the various media and be aware of their expectations.

The role of the public relations practitioner

 **Exercise**

Describe, in your own words, the role of public relations in an organisation. Compare your description with the following discussion.

Management and technical roles

Public relations fulfils two roles in an organisation, namely a management role and a technical role. What does this imply?

The management role refers to the advice and guidance the public relations practitioner gives to management on certain issues. For example, the public relations practitioner is best qualified to identify the most appropriate media to use for an important public announcement. To fulfil this role satisfactorily, it is imperative that the public relations practitioner has sufficient knowledge of the different media available and also knows how to approach them. Opportunities for the organisation to get positive publicity often arise. If the media is not approached and used correctly, these opportunities may be lost!

The public relations practitioner's technical role implies a responsibility for writing articles and news releases; collecting, editing and writing reports and articles for internal and external house magazines and annual reports; page layout; preparing audiovisual presentations; photography; media liaison; and so on.

Since these aspects form the core of the journalistic skills needed by the public relations practitioner, the focus in this book is on the public relations practitioner's technical role.

B Journalism

Definition of journalism

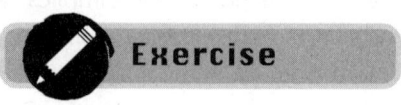

> Describe in your own words, the meaning of the term 'journalism'. Compare your description to the one given below.

Newsworthy: describes information of public interest

*'Journalism involves identifying **newsworthy** information for the mass communication.'*

Although this definition describes the essence of journalism, there is much more to the profession than meets the eye. Journalism involves two activities — gathering news and writing news — and both are dealt with in detail in this book. One can also add the identification of news as an initial step, after which more information is gathered (usually in the field) and the report is then written (or captured on the computer in the newsroom).

Identifying, gathering and writing news are interdependent and of equal importance to the media. Journalists need to develop a 'sense for news' and should be able to generate news stories on their own, apart from the news stories that are assigned to them.

The purpose of journalism

> Describe, in your own words, the purpose of journalism.

Compare your description with the following discussion.

Journalism concerns itself with gathering and conveying news to a large, diverse audience through the media, whether print (newspapers, magazines, etc) or electronic (radio, television, Internet, etc). Most people want to gain knowledge and become aware of national and international events. The media satisfy these needs most appropriately because of the variety of information they convey.

The media employ full-time journalists to fulfil this function but also use freelance journalists. A freelance journalist is a person who does not work for a specific media organisation. These journalists gather news on their own initiative and present newsworthy reports to various media who then pay them for their contributions. The media receive further information from several national and international *news agencies*. These include the South African Press Association (SAPA), Reuters, Sky News, Cable News Network (CNN) and so on. Journalists often rewrite or change these news items before presenting them in the style of their medium.

News agency: employs journalists who gather a wide variety of news for distribution to national and international mass communication media

Journalism usually implies one-way communication conveying information to the general public, be it readers (newspapers, magazines, etc), viewers (television) or listeners (radio). However, letters to the editors in the print media and 'phone-in' programmes or panel discussions in the electronic media establish two-way communication channels.

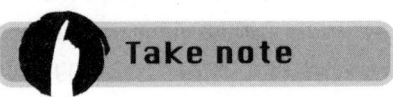

Take note

Journalism concerns itself with informing the general public, whereas public relations is all about informing internal and external target groups.

The role of the journalist

How do the media gather news? The central media figure is the journalist. The media use trained journalists to gather and present newsworthy information.

A *journalist's* or reporter's (the terms are synonymous) main responsibility is to identify and gather newsworthy information and to present it in a clear and understandable way through the media (print or electronic). The journalist's aim is, therefore, to convey important information to the general public using the mass communication media as channels of communication.

Journalists receive instructions from the news editor and also gather news on their own initiative. Normally, they keep a list of possible sources. Journalists gather information in several ways including personal or telephone interviews, *news releases, news conferences*, and so on. Although the print media employ professional photographers, it often happens that journalists themselves take photographs to accompany their reports or articles. A cameraperson accompanies the television journalist to capture visual effects.

Journalists' work is of such a nature that they are not bound to the office or normal office hours. They need to go out regularly to cover events in their effort to obtain information. They can, however, also conduct interviews on their office telephone.

Telephone interviews are the exception rather than the rule because the journalist visiting the scene of an event gathers more information. Journalists work under great pressure to meet their medium's deadline.

The style and nature of the different media determine the manner in which journalists execute their duty. A journalist at a small, local newspaper may be responsible for news reports varying from front-page lead stories to back-page sports news. Journalists at a large daily newspaper may have their own *beat* and be responsible for only political, court or sports reporting, etc.

Journalists need good interviewing skills to ensure that they elicit the correct information for publication or broadcast. They also need proficient writing skills and should be conversant in all aspects of the language in which they present their reports. Having obtained the facts, they present/write the report in an objective and unbiased manner. (*We discuss the way in which the journalist gathers information and presents reports for the various media [print and electronic] in later chapters.*)

Journalists should be professional at all times, acting responsibly and bearing *ethical* standards in mind.

News release: information concerning news-worthy events in an organisation, written in a specific format by a public relations practitioner and issued to the media

A news conference: the issue of newsworthy information to a gathering of media representatives

Beat: a specific field or area covered by specialist reporters, eg crime or sport

Ethical: according to a set of moral principles accepted by society

Although newspapers and radio and television stations employ journalists, many large companies also employ them to produce their internal and external house publications. Major corporations, such as financial banks, use their own journalists. Organisations who do not employ journalists use freelancers or a public relations practitioner to fill this role.

C Duties of the two professions — public relations and journalism

Now that we have briefly discussed the definitions, roles and purposes of the public relations practitioner and the journalist, let us look at their duties

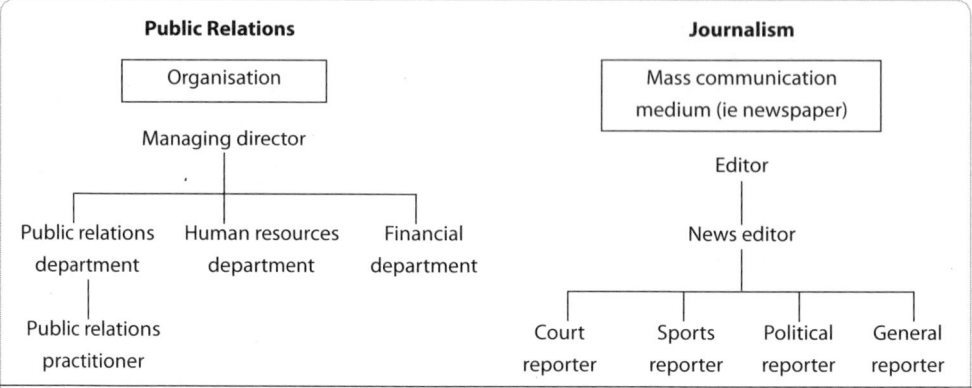

Public Relations

Organisation

Managing director

Public relations department   Human resources department   Financial department

Public relations practitioner

Journalism

Mass communication medium (ie newspaper)

Editor

News editor

Court reporter   Sports reporter   Political reporter   General reporter

Duties

1. Builds image of organisation
2. Liaises with management
3. Writes news releases
4. Addresses audiences
5. Gathers information for internal and external house publications
6. Writes articles for internal and external house publications
7. Produces publications (editing, photography, layout)
8. Prepares audiovisual presentations
9. Conducts research (public opinion/articles)
10. Liaises with media (supplying information/media enquiries)
11. Arranges news conferences
12. Establishes two-way communication channels
13. Interviews (for own publications/interviewed by journalists)
14. Arranges special events (open days, exhibitions, etc)
15. Rewrites information received to comply with the style and nature of in-house publications

Duties

1. Identifies newsworthy information
2. Contacts various news sources (news gathering)
3. Attends meetings, news conferences, seminars, social functions, etc
4. Conducts research for background information
5. Interviews sources
6. Takes photographs and writes captions for photographs
7. Writes reports and articles of various kinds
8. Rewrites news releases and news reports received from news agencies
9. (Depending on the size of newspaper) edits reports and articles and writes headlines
10. (Depending on the size of the newspaper) does page layout

Figure 1.2   The duties of public relations practitioners and journalists

 **Summary**

This chapter provides a broad overview of public relations and journalism to enable you to differentiate between the purposes and roles of the public relations practitioner and the journalist. The main aims of public relations are to build the image of an organisation and to establish effective two-way communication channels with internal and external target groups. The public relations practitioner fulfils a management and technical role in the organisation. The technical role corresponds with skills applied in journalism.

Journalists gather newsworthy information and present it in an understandable way to a large audience through the media. Journalism is directed at external target groups with little or no two-way communication, although journalists use two-way communication extensively in gathering information.

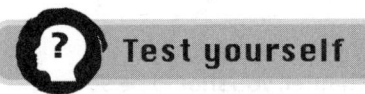 **Test yourself**

Answer the following questions to evaluate your understanding of this chapter.

1. Define the term 'public relations'.

2. Define the term 'journalism'.

3. What is the purpose of public relations? List the two roles the public relations practitioner plays in an organisation, and give a brief explanation of each.

4. What is the purpose of journalism?

5. Explain the role of the journalist employed by the media.

6. Which public relations role listed in question 3 corresponds with journalistic skills? Support your answer by providing reasons.

Sources consulted

Cutlip, SM, Center, AH & Broom, GM (1994) *Effective Public Relations*, Englewood Cliffs: Prentice Hall, Inc.

Lubbe, BA & Puth, G (1994) *Public Relations in South Africa: A Management Reader*, Durban: Butterworths.

Skinner, C & Von Essen, L (1995) *The Handbook of Public Relations*, Halfway House: Southern Book Publishers.

CHAPTER

2

Combining public relations and journalism in Media Studies

Objectives

After you have studied this chapter, you should be able to:

▶ discuss how public relations and journalism interact with each other; and

▶ discuss in detail how the public relations practitioner applies journalistic skills in executing his/her technical role.

Introduction

Publication: information printed in newspapers/ magazines

Broadcasting: the information aired to listeners (radio) and/ or viewers (television/ Internet)

It is clear from Chapter 1 that public relations and journalism are two unique occupations. In this chapter you will see how they depend on each other to fulfil their daily tasks.

As part of their technical role, public relations practitioners deal with the media. They use the mass communication media (newspapers, magazines, radio, television, etc) to obtain positive publicity for their organisations. They supply journalists with newsworthy information for *publication* or *broadcasting*. Conversely, journalists obtain a vast amount of news of public interest for the media from public relations practitioners in different organisations.

Interaction between public relations and journalism

Public relations practitioners need the media (print and electronic) to publish or broadcast organisational information to obtain positive publicity and to make the organisation known to the public. How do they do this?

One of the most important functions of the public relations practitioner is to establish good *media relations*. Public relations practitioners should know how the various media function and who they should contact to convey information. (See Part II for discussion on this aspect.)

Media relations: a relationship of mutual need between journalists and public relations practitioners

The public relations practitioner issues newsworthy information in various ways to the media, for example, a news release. Journalists will rewrite the news release to suit their specific medium's *style* and *nature*. Public relations practitioners also arrange news conferences where journalists gather to receive information first hand. The news conference also gives journalists an opportunity to raise specific questions. Public relations practitioners can also disseminate news through e-mail, personal contact or telephone interviews with journalists. It is important that public relations practitioners know the needs of the different media to improve their chances of publication or broadcasting. (Print and electronic media requirements are discussed in Part II.)

Style and nature: a specific way of writing/ presenting information for different media (print/electronic)

It is clear from the above that public relations practitioners will not get media coverage without the help of journalists. At the same time, public relations practitioners greatly assist journalists in obtaining news. Journalists might contact employees at an organisation for information. However, this is not a healthy situation because employees are not trained to deal with the media. It is therefore important that public relations practitioners make themselves known to journalists as their organisations' official spokespeople. Public relations practitioners, therefore, act as links between the organisations' management and journalists.

Often there is tension between public relations practitioners and journalists. Reasons for this include public relations practitioners being unavailable or not being competent to issue information. In these cases, journalists often contact other employees for information. It is the duty of public relations practitioners to deal with the media on behalf of management. Journalists should also know that public relations practitioners should be their first contact for information. Journalists who need to interview an organisation's employees should still use the public relations practitioner as their first contact. The public relations practitioner will arrange the interview.

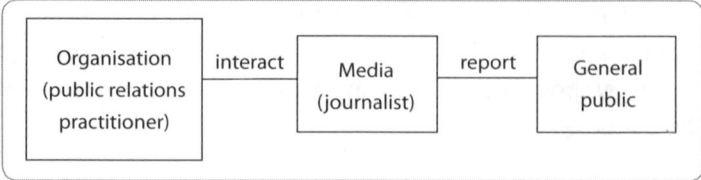

Figure 2.1 The interaction between public relations and journalism

If we review the duties of public relations practitioners and journalists listed in figure 2.1, we should be able to get a clearer picture of how they work together.

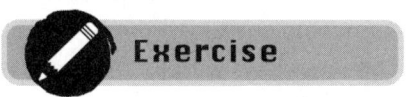

Page back to chapter 1 (figure 1.2) where the duties of public relations practitioners and journalists are listed. First list the duties you think illustrate their interaction. Then compare your list with the list of duties below.

Public relations: _____

_____

_____

_____

Journalism: _____

_____

_____

Public relations	Journalism

▶ writing *news releases*; and
 	
▶ liaising with the media by:
   ▶ supplying information and acting on enquiries;
   ▶ arranging news conferences; and
   ▶ granting interviews to the journalist.
	▶ rewriting news releases received from the public relations practitioner;
	
	▶ identifying newsworthy information by contacting the public relations practitioner who acts as news source;
	
	▶ interviewing the public relations practitioner; and
	
	▶ attending news conferences, meetings, seminars, etc to *gather information*.

The above exercise illustrates how public relations and journalism interact to inform the general public about newsworthy events.

Journalistic skills needed by the public relations practitioner

In the previous section we saw how public relations and journalism work together. In this section we focus on the journalistic skills public relations practitioners need to fulfil their technical roles.

Before we discuss the journalistic skills applied in public relations, do the following exercise to see if you can pinpoint these journalistic skills.

Interact: depend on each other to execute a task, ie the public relations practitioner gives information **to** the journalist/journalist seeks information **from** public relations practitioner

Exercise

Use the list of public relations and journalistic duties in chapter 1 (figure 1.2) for this exercise. By comparing the duties of public relations practitioners and journalists, list the duties of public relations corresponding with those of journalism to establish the journalistic skills required for public relations.

For example:

Public relations practitioners:

Journalists:

Gather information for internal and external house publications

Contact various news sources (news gathering)

Here we see that the journalist identifies newsworthy information and uses various news sources to gather information. The same skill is applied by the public relations practitioner in gathering information for organisational publications.

Now, by following the above example, see what other journalistic skills are applicable in public relations

Compare your list with the skills given below:

Public relations practitioners

▶ conduct interviews;

▶ write articles for their own publications;

▶ produce publications that require editing, page layout, photography;

▶ conduct research for articles; and

▶ rewrite information received to comply with the style and nature of in-house publications.

When compared with journalists, we find the following corresponding duties:

Journalists

▶ interview sources;

▶ write news reports and articles;

▶ edit news reports and articles;

▶ do page layout;

▶ take photographs;

▶ conduct research for background information; and

▶ rewrite news releases and other stories received from sources.

What is significant about this list? Have you noticed that most of the skills applied in journalism — especially from the print media — are needed in public relations?

 **Take note**

The above similarities show how strong the link between public relations and journalism is. It shows how important journalistic skills are for the public relations practitioner establishing publications for internal and external use.

The following example shows how public relations practitioners use these journalistic skills:

Public relations practitioners need to publish an internal house magazine. They identify newsworthy information and contact various sources for this. Research is done to obtain background information and interviews are conducted to gather further information. They then write the articles and rewrite other contributions. Photographs they have taken accompany certain articles. They edit all reports, articles and photographs, and arrange them for page layout. They then do the page layout for the various reports, articles and photographs. This is done manually or with the help of a desktop publishing program. (How public relations practitioners acquire these journalistic skills is discussed in Part 3.)

Our example of journalistic activities concentrated on the print media (newspapers/magazines) where most of the journalistic skills required by public relations practitioners are applied. When comparing the activities of journalists from the print media with those of the electronic media, namely radio and television, there are still many similarities, eg news gathering, interviewing, editing, writing, etc. The difference, however, is in the way journalists from different media handle and present their news reports. For example, television interviews and reports are edited on videotape and combined with text written for the newsreader. In Part 2, where the various media are discussed, we look more closely at how journalists from these different media handle and present their news reports.

Summary

In this chapter, we have seen how public relations and journalism interact with each other. We have shown how public relations uses journalism to convey information to the general public and how journalism uses public relations to obtain news of public interest. The public relations practitioner acts as a link between the organisation and the journalist. To ensure that their facts are correct, journalists should contact an organisation's public relations practitioner — not other employees.

Many similarities exist between journalistic skills applied by the journalist and journalistic skills applied by the public relations practitioner. The journalist applies these skills to have newsworthy events published or broadcast to a diverse, general public. The same skills applied by the public relations practitioner enable him/her to produce internal publications aimed at employees and external publications aimed at specific target groups.

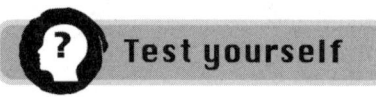

Test yourself

Answer the following questions to evaluate your understanding of this chapter:

1. Give reasons why journalism forms an important part of Media Studies for the public relations practitioner.

2. Explain how public relations and journalism interact with each other. Give appropriate examples.

3. Explain why the public relations practitioner needs journalistic skills and give an example of how these are applied in public relations.

4. Discuss the skills needed by both public relations practitioners and journalists.

CHAPTER
3

News and public relations

Objectives

After you have studied this chapter, you should be able to:

▶ define the term 'news';
▶ list the characteristics of news;
▶ understand news values;
▶ discuss the types and categories of news;
▶ identify appropriate, newsworthy issues in an organisation for the mass communication media;
▶ identify appropriate, newsworthy issues in an organisation for internal house (in-house) publications; and
▶ identify news sources appropriate in certain situations for the:
  ▶ journalist; and
  ▶ the public relations practitioner.

Introduction

In chapter 2, the importance of the interaction between public relations practitioners and journalists became quite obvious. It is also clear that this interaction is ongoing and that a sound relationship between public relations practitioners and the media is invaluable.

One of the main results of effective interaction between these two professions is the benefit both can derive from it, provided it is handled correctly. Publishing news of an organisation in the media accomplishes the following two objectives:

⦁ media publicity is enjoyed by the organisation; and

⦁ an opportunity for the journalist/media to provide fresh, important or interesting information (news) to the public is realised.

The public relations practitioner acts as an important source of news to the media by providing timely information about newsworthy issues. But:

> **HOW** do public relations practitioners know what is newsworthy?
>
> **WHERE** do they look for news?
>
> **HOW** do they identify newsworthy issues; and
>
> **HOW** do they establish to *whom* and *how* this news should be conveyed?

The answers to these questions are important to public relations practitioners. Once accustomed to finding news and dealing with the media, they will be able to correctly identify and channel news to the various media with the most effective results.

In this chapter, we look at what journalists regard as news. We also establish the characteristics, the types of and categories of news. We then explain how public relations practitioners can apply this knowledge to identify news in their organisations. In the last part of the chapter, we discuss the various ways in which news is identified and how information is gathered by journalists and public relations practitioners.

Part 2 of this book deals with how the public relations practitioner decides to whom and in what fashion the news should be conveyed.

What is news?

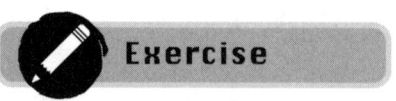 **Exercise**

> *Describe, in your own words, what news is.*

Compare your answer with the following:

It is not easy to define news. Definitions of news vary from 'news is what newspapers publish', to 'news is what the public wants to know'. Hough (1995:1) says: 'News is what people need or want to know, whatever interests them, whatever adds to their knowledge and understanding of the world around them. News is also what a reporter or an editor at any particular moment considers interesting or exciting or important — something that the reporter or editor thinks will interest or be useful to readers.'

Let us take a look at a few comments from South African news media people:

▶ Reporter — television news: 'News is what the public has the right to know.'
▶ Editor — local newspaper: 'News is interesting or important information aimed at the local community.'
▶ Reporter — Sunday newspaper: 'Our readers determine what news is — news is often of a controversial nature.'

Take note

In the light of these observations, we can formulate our own **general** definition of news, namely:

'News comprises current issues or events that have credibility and are important or of interest to the public.'

Characteristics of news

Although definitions of 'news' vary considerably, one or more of the following *characteristics* will always be present:

Characteristics: typical or distinct attributes of newsworthy events

▶ news is *new* (when one is made aware of an issue or event for the first time) or it will add a new *angle* or perspective to already known information;
▶ news is *interesting* and/or *important*; and
▶ news is *credible*.

Angle: a written news report's focus or point of departure

Further criteria determine the newsworthiness of an event. It must be different, unique or exceptional in some way. Think here in terms of something tragic, strange, ironic, unusual, the latest, most expensive, controversial, pioneering, important, significant, and so on.

Exercise

Choose two news reports from any newspaper or television/radio news bulletin. Identify the 'newsworthy' characteristics of the reports (as described on the previous page). Motivate why you regard the reports as newsworthy by explaining the characteristics you have found.

CHARACTERISTIC	MOTIVATION
News report 1	
News report 2	

News values

What makes one story more newsworthy than another? In media terms, we refer to this as 'news values' — a checklist of sorts that helps determine the newsworthiness of a story. Lieb (2009: 26–27) identifies the following basic news values:

Impact

The primary measure of the value of any information is its impact or effect on the audience. An increase in the price of petrol in South Africa would have a *direct* impact on the people. Journalists believe that direct impact is the most important aspect of newsworthiness.

A flood in Johannesburg will only have an impact on the people living in the area and on those who may have family/friends living there. This is known as *indirect* impact.

However, should the floods cause great damage to the maize crops, it could also indirectly affect many more people (possibility because of possible price increases).

Prominence

As we know, names make news — the bigger the name, the bigger the news. Celebrities, politicians and other famous people catch the attention of the public. However, too much focus on prominence can lead to overblown coverage of the insignificant actions of minor celebrities.

Currency

News is one of the oldest examples of recycling. Topics that are popular today will disappear and then reappear months or years later. This cycle is fuelled largely by the focus on unusual events. When something strange and dramatic occurs, it attracts attention to similar events and underlying conditions. For example, when a national study finds that recent strike action by educators has compromised the tertiary student intake, journalists will ask why and they will pay more attention to related stories. Those subsequent reports have *currency* — a direct tie to stories already in the news. Over time, another topic will take centre stage and the cycle will start all over again.

Conflict

Most interesting news stories are based on some sort of conflict: people battling nature, other people, themselves, disease and so on. Stories about political conflicts, war and crime are the more popular news stories.

Timeliness

News must be fresh — today's news is stale tomorrow. With today's online newsrooms, stories are continuously updated and thus print editions need to ensure that their information is current at the time of publication.

Unusualness

New stories tend to focus on things that are out of the ordinary. Unfortunately, *unusualness* can lead journalists to ignore important stories and focus instead on insubstantial ones.

A local gardener who grows a pumpkin in the shape of the President is more likely to get coverage than a story about the many people in the same community who go hungry every night.

Proximity

Proximity refers to physical nearness. People like to read or hear news about people and events that are close to them. The closer an issue or an event is to the readers, the greater is its impact and news value.

Affinity

People are interested in other people who share characteristics or have an *affinity* with them (religion, nationality, race and so on). For example, stories involving the Pope would be considered more newsworthy in an area with a significant Roman Catholic population than in an area primarily populated by Baptists.

Human interest

Stories that have a strong emotional content are said to have *human interest*. Some, like a story about a half-blind dog saving the life of a farmer who had raised her, makes the audience feel good and help offset heavy and often downbeat news. This is also sometimes valued too highly, leading to important stories being pushed out of the news by emotional stories of little consequence.

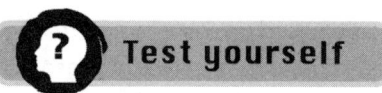

Test yourself

Read through the articles in the front page of any newspaper. Make a list of the news values you find in each article.

Types of news

News report: report on newsworthy events written and/or presented by a journalist for the media

We distinguish between two main *types* of news, namely *hard news* and *soft news*. Hard news stories are of a current and immediate nature and are usually found in the more important pages of a newspaper. Hard news stories carry important news, especially of a political, economic or crime-related nature. They also cover traumatic stories or events affecting media consumers, eg changes in the government, petrol price increases, mass murders, natural disasters, etc. These stories are usually of a serious nature and are of regional, national and/or international importance or interest.

Soft news stories include features that lend a human perspective to hard news. They are 'follow-ups' to hard news stories, eg political, economic and crime stories, focusing on their human dimension. Humorous stories, 'women's page' stories, art stories, etc are examples of soft news.

A television news bulletin will begin with hard news stories on violence, crime, political issues, and so on, and end on a lighter note with a story on, for example, the birth of a baby elephant at a zoo. Many newspapers also carry a story in a lighter vein on the front page to break away from the hard news.

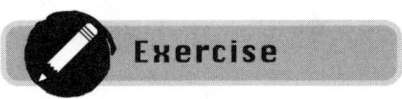 **Exercise**

> Take any newspaper and choose a hard-news story and a soft-news story. Summarise the content of each story and motivate your choice for each.

It is also necessary to know that we distinguish between scheduled and unscheduled news and expected and unexpected news. These differences can be explained by the following example:

▶ The public relations practitioner invites journalists to cover an expected event, eg the unveiling of a plaque. Journalists *schedule* the date and time of this event.

▶ An underground explosion at a mine is *unexpected* and is therefore *unscheduled* news. The explosion is unpredictable and the journalist cannot schedule the event.

Categories of news

News is also classified in different *categories*. The media apply these categories differently. Think of the timeslots given to sport and weather in a television news bulletin and compare them with the news distribution in a daily newspaper. A few major news categories are:

Categories: classification of newsworthy events

▶ *Politics*: news from parliament, political leaders, local government;

> *Finances*: stock exchange, gold price, annual budgets, major companies;
> *Planning and development*: new schools, hospitals, dams;
> *Sport*: soccer, rugby, tennis, cricket, netball;
> *Weather*: first snow in winter, severe drought, flood;
> *Crime*: murder, robbery, fraud;
> *Emergencies*: disasters, tragedies;
> *Human interest*: people, animals; and
> *Personalities*: public figures such as members of parliament, the captains of sports teams, etc.

News can also be categorised into events or issues of local, regional, national and international interest. The main theme of an event or issue will determine its news category.

Now that we know how to identify newsworthy events by observing the characteristics, types and categories of news and news values, we will discuss how this is important to public relations.

Public relations and news

Why is it important for the public relations practitioner to know what news is? Because this knowledge will enable the public relations practitioner to guide management, not only in disseminating information of importance to the media, but also by contacting the media at the right time for the right reasons.

Every day the media is inundated with information from public relations practitioners. Unfortunately, it too often happens that much of this information cannot be used, the main reason being that public relations practitioners are often uncertain or do not know what the media considers newsworthy. In conveying information to the media, the public relations practitioner must ensure that the information is newsworthy and of public interest. For example, a major petroleum company's change of corporate identity is newsworthy and of public interest, and should be conveyed to the media. In contrast, the promotion of a clerk to the rank of senior clerk in an organisation generates no public interest and should not be conveyed to the media. However, if the clerk is a well-known sportsperson, his/her promotion might be considered newsworthy.

Although the aim of public relations practitioners is to get publicity for their organisation, they must guard against management pressure to inform the media of general issues and events for the sake of publicity only — thereby ignoring the stories' newsworthiness.

> **Taking cognisance of 'what news is' will enhance management's and the public relations practitioner's professional approach to disseminating newsworthy information to the media. By not being able to distinguish between what is newsworthy and what is not, they will develop an unfavourable reputation with the media.**

Public relations practitioners should know that journalists are able to obtain information from several sources. If the public relations practitioner does not act proactively and inform journalists of events immediately, the chances are good that the journalist will obtain the information elsewhere.

The public relations practitioner will then have to act reactively in giving the organisation's side of the story. Public relations practitioners should not wait for journalists to contact them for information — they should break news to the media immediately. Should there be a strike at an organisation, the public relations practitioner should immediately make the media aware of the situation. By waiting for journalists to initiate contact, the assumption could be drawn that the organisation is hiding facts regarding the strike and journalists may try to get their information from employees. A timely *tip-off* to journalists can benefit media relations.

Tip-off: information that leads to a news story

Public relations practitioners should also be aware that various media value news differently. For example, toxic waste from a plant threatening nearby residents' lives will be front-page news in the local newspaper. The level of toxicity and the threat posed by the waste will determine the news value a daily newspaper ascribes to the report. Depending on the seriousness (newsworthiness) of such an incident, it might be included in a radio news programme, or even a television news bulletin. When disseminating newsworthy information to the media, the public relations practitioner also has to choose the correct medium for the message.

Remembering that the public relations practitioner is responsible for conveying organisational information to internal and external target groups, the following definition of news is appropriate to *public relations*:

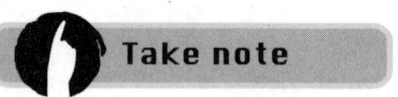

> *News is information that is current, important and of interest to the specific public it is aimed at, be it an external/general public interested in general, 'everyday' news or an internal public (employees) demanding its own, distinct type of news.*

Target groups (external and internal) for the public relations practitioner

Target groups in the general public

Who is the general public? This public consists of 'everybody out there'. In other words, in conveying information through the mass communication media, the intention is to reach a wide range of people, from schoolchildren to high-ranking government officials or businesspeople.

Various target groups important to the organisation are identified in the general public, eg clients, community and opinion leaders. These target groups can be reached by means other than the media when specific messages need to be conveyed to them. External house magazines, annual reports, etc are used for this purpose.

The general public, as an external target group, is important to the public relations practitioner because the public shapes opinion towards the organisation.

Public opinion

Public opinion is formed by what the general public reads, hears and sees of an organisation in the media. Although the main aim of public relations is to build a positive public opinion towards the organisation by having positive news published or broadcast in the media, it is also necessary to face any negative news about it. By providing the media with both good and bad news, the public relations practitioner will gain more credibility with the media and, ultimately, the general public.

The honest revelation of facts about the organisation through the media will have positive, long-term benefits.

Employees as the internal target group

Public relations practitioners should bear in mind that they are also responsible for identifying internal news and that, although certain issues are not valued by the media and the outside public, they are important to the internal target group.

Employees need a distinct type of news. Hardly any news communicated internally through the in-house newsletter reaches the media, even though it is important *news* to the internal public. In identifying news for employees, the same criteria that apply to the media apply to internal publications. Employees want to read a publication containing new information (or additional new information) that is interesting and important. Hard and soft news stories should be included. In categorising the information, public relations practitioners should be satisfied that they have provided the employees with a wide range of newsworthy information.

Any news about an organisation will interest employees. Matters concerning policy, internal structures, rules, regulations, general company issues, as well as interesting and successful employees, are important news and should be communicated to employees. The media might find issues, such as the visit of an important overseas dignitary to the organisation, interesting enough to publish or broadcast it.

 **Take note**

It must be remembered that all information should be communicated to the employees before it is conveyed to the media.

33

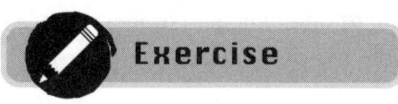

Exercise

> *Look at the following examples of organisational events. Choose items that you consider to be of importance or interest to the readers of:*
>
> *(1)   an internal newsletter (employees only); and*
>
> *(2)   the mass communication media (general public).*
>
> ▶ *crèche facilities for employees' children;*
>
> ▶ *the appointment of a new executive director;*
>
> ▶ *the discovery of fraud in the company;*
>
> ▶ *the imminent opening of a new branch;*
>
> ▶ *the destruction of an important section of head office;*
>
> ▶ *negotiations and a possible takeover of a similar organisation abroad;*
>
> ▶ *the annual award ceremony for employees;*
>
> ▶ *the organisation's annual sports day;*
>
> ▶ *the election of a new committee for the organisation's social club;*
>
> ▶ *a strike by employees due to a salary dispute;*
>
> ▶ *a visit by a foreign dignitary to an organisation; or*
>
> ▶ *an improved medical aid scheme for employees.*

News sources

Now that we have discussed various facts around the meaning of the term 'news', the following question must be asked: 'Where do we find news?'

News sources: sources used to identify and/or gather information of news value

This question brings us to the importance of *news sources*. To enable us to identify news and to *obtain facts and information needed to write or present the news report*, we need *reliable* news sources.

News sources are indispensable to journalists and public relations practitioners searching for news and information. Without these sources, factual and correct information will be difficult to find.

Take note

> *Although there are many news sources available to the journalist and the public relations practitioner, the most important thing to remember is that each incident, event or issue will determine the relevant news source.*

In this section, we will firstly look at the general news sources useful to the *journalist* and secondly, at the news sources useful to the *public relations practitioner*.

News sources for journalists of the mass media

The *journalist* finds hints for possible news stories from various areas. All journalists have a list of established contacts that they use to find news stories and gather information, eg the police, the fire brigade, the traffic department, hospitals, government departments, transitional council offices, etc. Although the public relations practitioner of the specific institution usually acts as the spokesperson (this is advisable), journalists may have other contacts in these institutions. Public relations practitioners will often find this to be the case, and it is very difficult to control.

Journalists also get 'news tips' or tip-offs from members of the public, from employees of organisations and from emergency radio services. News reports carried by other media can also be followed up in an effort to obtain a new angle to a story.

Apart from news stories assigned to them by the news editor, journalists use several other sources for stories. These include:

▶ public meetings or speeches;
▶ news conferences;
▶ news releases;
▶ annual reports/budgets;
▶ social functions; and
▶ news agencies, eg Associated Press (AP) and South African Press Association (SAPA).

Once a news story is identified, journalists make use of every possible source to obtain adequate and accurate information.

Eye-witnesses, spokespersons of organisations, members of the public, emergency services, pressure groups, etc can all be considered major sources of news. If this is not sufficient, they might use additional source material, including:

▶ court reports;
▶ media reports;
▶ public records;
▶ databases/archives;
▶ libraries;
▶ museums;
▶ press clippings;
▶ other publications; and
▶ the Internet.

The following example illustrates the use of news sources by a journalist:

> An aeroplane crash is announced on an emergency radio service. The news is *identified*. The sources a journalist may use to *gather information* for the news report include:
>
> ▶ spokesperson/public relations practitioner from the airline;
> ▶ emergency services (ambulance, fire brigade, rescue teams);
> ▶ the police investigating officers;
> ▶ relatives of the passengers;
> ▶ eyewitnesses, the airport's control room staff;
> ▶ hospitals receiving injured passengers; and
> ▶ survivors of the crash (if any).

Because public relations practitioners act as very important news sources for journalists, we need to see how they can assist the journalist in identifying news and gathering information on a specific organisation.

The public relations practitioner as a news source

Public relations practitioners act as news sources for the media in several ways, the most common of which is issueing news releases to the various media. Another way is to arrange a news conference if the event, incident or situation warrants it. Information is also conveyed through personal (face-to-face) or telephone interviews with journalists. Public relations practitioners gain publicity for the organisation in their role as news source, which, unlike advertisements, is free.

It is important to note that equipment, eg a *telephone*, is a *resource* (aid) used to reach a news source and *not a news source*. The same applies to an interview — it is the *person* with whom the interview is conducted that is a *news source*.

When acting as a news source, one of the most important lessons to learn is that public relations practitioners should never favour one journalist or medium. When publicising a newsworthy event, public relations practitioners must inform the journalists of all the relevant media simultaneously. It is up to the media to decide whether they are interested in the story.

There are, however, certain situations in which public relations practitioners should use their own judgement. For example, it might happen that a journalist hears of an incident in the organisation and approaches the public relations practitioner for comment. Perhaps, owing to the sensitivity of the incident, the public relations practitioner (in conjunction with management) initially had no intention of making the incident public knowledge. When approached for comment, public relations practitioners should not try to suppress information and should never say: 'No comment!'

In such cases, careful consideration should be given to whether the information will be relayed to that journalist alone or whether it will be made known to other media as well. Since journalists thrive on *scoops*, the decision might be taken to give the journalist his or her moment of glory before revealing the information to other media.

Scoop: first report of a news event

Once the information is publicised by the journalist, the public relations practitioner should have additional information ready for other journalists seeking a fresh angle to the story.

If the intention was to make the information known to the general media, the public relations practitioner should advise the journalist accordingly, so that the journalist is aware that his or her medium will not be the only carrier of the news.

News sources for the public relations practitioner

Now that we know from where and how the journalist gets news and how the public relations practitioner can act as a news source, we look at the public relations practitioner's news sources. Keep in mind that public relations practitioners are only concerned with news relevant to their *own organisations* and that their duty is twofold, namely to inform their internal *and* external public about happenings in their organisations.

Many of the news sources used by journalists can also be used by the public relations practitioner. These include:

⦁ databases/archives;
⦁ other publications;
⦁ libraries;
⦁ museums;
⦁ annual reports;
⦁ press clippings; and
⦁ the Internet.

Sources used more often by the public relations practitioner include the following:

⦁ own staff;
⦁ meetings;
⦁ minutes of meetings;
⦁ management;
⦁ internal publications;
⦁ previous/retired employees;
⦁ other relevant organisations; and
⦁ shareholders of the organisation.

The same criteria that apply to journalists apply here, namely that the event or incident will determine the sources used to obtain information. What is important for the public relations practitioner in selecting news sources is that the type of organisation will also determine the sources that can be used. For example, a public relations practitioner at a hospital may have to gather information from patients or a public relations practitioner in local government may find that information is needed from ratepayers, etc.

The following is an example of how public relations practitioners use news sources:

A major hotel group plans to build a multimillion-rand hotel complex. The public relations practitioner may identify this newsworthy information in the minutes of a meeting and through discussions with management. The sources that the public relations practitioner can use to gather information for a news release include architects' drawings and presentations, financial statements, management's decisions and comments, etc.

These are some examples of sources that can be used, but public relations practitioners might find other sources relevant to their specific needs.

It is clear that in order to identify newsworthy events and to gather more information for internal and external house publications as well as for the media, the public relations practitioner uses several sources.

The public relations practitioner uses news sources to gather information for a news release or a news conference. Since these are ways in which the public relations practitioner acts as a news source for the media (as discussed in the previous section), news releases and news conferences are not news sources for the public relations practitioner. The only time the public relations practitioner can use a news release as a news source is when background information of an event was covered by an earlier news release(s).

▶ Select news sources suitable for the public relations practitioner searching for information about the company's centenary celebrations.
▶ Select news sources that a journalist of a local, weekly newspaper can use to find three news stories for the week's edition. Identify the type of stories to explain your sources.

> ▶ Select news sources a journalist can use to write a front-page story about an earthquake.
>
> ▶ Select news sources the public relations practitioner will use to write a news release about a staff member who was selected for the national soccer team for the forthcoming African Cup of Nations soccer trophy.

Creation of news

In addition to using news sources to identify and gather information on a newsworthy issue, news can also be created. For example, the public relations practitioner can create opportunities for news stories by organising special events such as open days, exhibitions, functions, etc.

Summary

In this chapter, we described the term 'news' as an issue or event that is current, interesting or important and of value to people. Two types of news were distinguished, namely hard news and soft news. There are several categories of news, eg crime, sport, etc.

The public relations practitioner's duty is to identify newsworthy events in the organisation that are of interest to the employees and/or the general public. Public relations practitioners use the media to convey information about their organisation to the general public and use internal publications to inform staff of events.

In the last part of this chapter, the various news sources the journalist uses to identify news and gather information and the way in which these can be used by the public relations practitioner, were discussed. Public relations practitioners are more limited in their choice of news sources than the journalist, since they are concerned only with news about their organisation. The event will, in each case, determine the sources used to gather information.

? Test yourself

1. Describe the term 'news':
    (a) from a journalist's point of view; and
    (b) from a public relations practitioner's point of view.

2. Choose any two news reports from a newspaper, a radio or a television news bulletin:
    (a) Discuss the characteristics present in every news report.
    (b) Choose the types of news involved in each report.
    (c) Select the categories of each report.

3. Identify at least three different newsworthy events in an organisation that the public relations practitioner can convey to:
    (a) the general public through the media; and
    (b) the employees of the organisation through a newsletter.

4. A journalist has to write a news report on a train disaster in which several passengers were killed and many injured. List and discuss the various sources the journalist can use to gather information.

5. A public relations practitioner has to write an article for the organisation's internal publication about the appointment of a new managing director. List and discuss the various sources that can be used to gather information.

6. An organisation has recently received unfavourable publicity in the media. In an effort to reverse the negative image created to a positive image, the public relations practitioner decides to create an opportunity for news that will portray the organisation in a favourable light. Discuss how the public relations practitioner can create news that will attract the attention of the media.

Sources consulted

Hough, GA (1995) *News Writing*, USA: Houghton Mifflin Company.

Lieb, T (2009) *All the News: Writing and Reporting for Convergent Media*, Boston: Pearson Education.

CHAPTER

4

Ethics in public relations and journalism

Objectives

After you have studied this chapter, you should be able to:

▶ explain the concepts 'moral' and 'legal' ethics; and
▶ distinguish between right and wrong in your conduct towards others when practising public relations.

Introduction

Ethics: the science of morals; moral principles, rules of conduct.

Now that we have established the interaction between public relations and journalism in the previous chapters, we need to pay attention to another very important aspect, namely *ethics*. While growing up, we were taught the difference between right and wrong in our conduct towards others. While we tend to strive towards upholding our cultural values and moral principles when dealing with others, we also need to be aware of what is acceptable to the broader community. In our professions we constantly have to make decisions regarding our interaction with others and we usually base those decisions on what we feel is the correct one for that moment. However, this is where ethics plays a major role since decisions made could be against a prescribed code of conduct. Although different occupational groups have their own code of conduct or professional standards, they basically all point to one thing, namely to be credible and to be respected by those with whom they come into contact. Communicators should encourage frequent communication and messages that are honest in their content, accurate and appropriate to the needs of the organisation and its audiences.

You should become acquainted with the full scope of ethics in public relations (Code of Professional Standards for the practice of Public Relations) as laid out by the Public Relations Institute of Southern Africa (PRISA) and we shall therefore not cover this issue in detail here. The focus of this chapter will be on the conduct of the public relations practitioner towards journalists.

As a public relations practitioner, you should be as aware of the moral and legal ethical pitfalls in the news media as the journalist is.

Moral and legal ethics are explained in detail later in this chapter. In short, moral ethics is concerned with goodness or badness of character or disposition, whereas legal ethics refers to rules recognised by law.

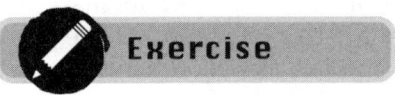

Before studying the rest of the chapter, read through the following fictitious scenario and answer the questions that follow (bearing in mind that the events in this scenario are very likely to occur in a real-life situation):

Joan had been a senior member of the PR department at a large hospital for three years. As the head of the department had resigned, she was filling the role of acting head in the hope of being promoted into the permanent position fairly soon. Joan had enjoyed a good standing with management and was highly respected by the staff and the public for her integrity, trustworthiness, knowledge and skills. She also had excellent relations with the media and was well respected by them.

As a member of the management team, Joan attended all management meetings. One such meeting turned out to be one that Joan may well have preferred not to have attended at all. At this meeting, the superintendent of the hospital announced that a young patient had died unexpectedly during the course of the previous night. Subsequent investigation revealed that the attending doctor may have been negligent and could be directly linked to the death of the patient. The doctor concerned, however, happened to be the superintendent's brother, who was only three months away from retirement. The family of the patient, in the meantime, had been informed that the child had died of natural causes.

Management felt that disclosing the facts could cause the hospital to face negative media publicity, while the doctor could even face dismissal so soon before his retirement. For these reasons, along with other repercussions that may arise, they decided to keep a tight lid on this sensitive issue. They specifically requested Joan not to divulge any of this to the media and should any journalist ask her directly, to deny any fault on the part of either the doctor or the hospital.

The following day Joan received a phone call from one of her journalist friends. He was calling to enquire whether there was any truth in the rumour that he had heard regarding the death of a patient due to a doctor's negligence. Torn between her instructions by management not to admit this to the media and her good reputation regarding truthfulness towards the media, Joan had to make a decision that could have a major effect on her present and future career at the hospital, as well as her relations with the media. She could admit it 'off the record' and request the journalist for 'friendship's sake' not to publish the story, she could disregard management's instruction and tell the truth or she could follow management's instructions and deny it.

Before Joan could make her decision, however, the journalist — suspecting that she may try to cover up the story — invited her to join him and a group of friends for an all-expenses-paid weekend at Sun City in exchange for information regarding this case. He was aware that she had never been to Sun City as she had once expressed a wish to visit this magnificent place. Once again, Joan was confronted with a very difficult choice.

Questions

1. If you were in Joan's shoes, how would you have acted:

    a) towards management's request in the first place?
    b) towards the journalist's very tempting exchange offer?

2. *What decision would you have made? Support your answer by providing reasons.*

3. *Discuss all the ethical dilemmas involved in this scenario: from management's actions and the decisions Joan is facing, up to the offer from the journalist. Consider the various options, weighing the rights and wrongs against one another.*

4. *If the journalist was willing to accept the 'off the record' information and kept to his undertaking not to publish the story, would you say his conduct was ethical? Support your answer by providing reasons.*

5. *In your opinion, is the offer of a free trip to Sun City in exchange for the information ethical? Support your answer by providing reasons.*

Facing moral ethics

Both the public relations practitioner and the journalist must realise that ethical dilemmas raise tough questions about the right of privacy and the public's right to know. Both must have credibility and must be respected by the various publics with whom they interact.

When dealing with situations that are difficult to categorise as definitely right or wrong, remember that your ultimate decision should be made with respect, competence and an active, creative imagination to arrive at positive ethical solutions. Although you can always refer to the written code of professional standards to support your decision making, you need to bear in mind that your decision may have implications that are not apparent from the written code. In accepting the code at face value, the needs and interests of the public always come first.

Public relations practitioners often have very difficult decisions to make, since they not only have to consider their own behaviour, but also that of the institution that they represent. If you refer back to the exercise scenario you will see that, should Joan choose the option to divulge the information to the media, she could not only jeopardise her chances of promotion, but could also even face dismissal. The hospital also has a good image and this one negative incident could

Moral ethics: the name given to our concern for good behaviour; an obligation to consider not only our own personal well-being but also that of society as a whole

harm the image that Joan had worked so hard at helping to create. Despite the impact on the hospital's image, Joan should be focusing on what is more important: her possible dismissal and the hospital receiving negative publicity, or silence in exchange for possible promotion and the hospital upholding its good name. One would obviously prefer to choose the latter, but is it right in view of ethical standards?

The best option for Joan would be to tell the journalist that she would investigate his inquiry and then to approach management, informing them that this rumour had reached the news media. In an effort to uphold management's and her own ethical standards she should persuade management to issue a news release to answer the inquiry, even though the doctor in question may face action and the hospital receive negative publicity. The main ethical direction here is to tell the truth and to provide an accurate picture.

The news media deserve honest and valid use of the channels — you should not involve them in compromising situations through, for example, lying or feeding them insignificant or incomplete information. The public relations practitioner should respond to the news media with a straightforward presentation of the facts, even when the story is unfavourable.

Another option Joan could have taken was to admit the story to the journalist but to request him not to divulge his source of information. By taking this route, Joan would have put the journalist in a difficult position, since he would then be confronted with the ethical question of when and how he should acknowledge the public relations practitioner as a source of news. The journalist should, on his part, employ discretion and good editorial judgement about what is disseminated and whether or not attribution should be withheld.

There was one more option open to Joan: that of accepting the journalist's offer of a trip to Sun City in exchange for information. Clearly, this is something that Joan should not even consider. The code of ethics states that the public relations practitioner may not receive compensation from the news media for disseminating information, nor may he or she offer compensation to a journalist for ensuring publicity.

A public relations practitioner should realise that the news media could be helpful but also harmful. You should not act on what is expected of you but rather be able to reflect on what is ethical.

In real life, it sometimes happens that the public relations practitioner wishes to thank the news media for publishing newsworthy events. Likewise, a journalist may wish to thank the practitioner for assistance in gathering news. In such cases, the exchange of small gifts is regarded as harmless and is perfectly acceptable. However, ethics will play a role where a gift to a public relations practitioner or to a journalist seems large enough to be potentially compromising.

From the above, it is clear how difficult ethical decisions can be. As a professional, however, you should always uphold the code of professional standards, even if it could jeopardise you and/or the institution you represent. As a public relations practitioner, you should always be aware of ethical pitfalls. If you are not certain how to act in certain situations and are not sure what the consequences of your actions might be, consult your professional body for assistance instead of getting yourself knee-deep in trouble.

It is also true, however, that what is ethical to one person is not necessarily ethical to another. The practice of ethics is interpreted not only from a personal viewpoint, but also from a cultural one. You may, therefore, sometimes find yourself making questionable decisions in response to the moral choices with which you are faced.

 **Exercise**

At the beginning of this chapter you were asked to answer questions based on a certain scenario. Go back to those answers and see if you still agree with your responses or if, after having studied this chapter, you would change any of them. Compare your answers with those of a friend and try to establish whether you have an understanding of what moral ethics involves.

Legal ethics and the public relations practitioner

Just as public relations practitioners have to know what is morally ethical in the normal carrying out of their duties, so, too, is it essential for them to understand that there are legal ethics that must be adhered to.

There are numerous legal issues which public relations practitioners may face in their daily work and an awareness of these is essential in order to prevent any harmful legal matters arising against them or the organisation they represent. They should therefore always act within the prescribed legal ethics. If, at any time, they have any doubts regarding the legality of an action, they should first consult the organisation's legal department for clarity and guidance.

Public relations practitioners must be careful not to write or say anything that may harm the reputation of another person. Even when an individual is a public figure, public relations practitioners must always consider the individual's right to privacy. Among the legal pitfalls of which they must be aware are defamation of character and the misuse of copyright materials.

Exercise

Let us look at another scenario that a public relations practitioner could face working for any company, whatever its size.

Miriam is the public relations practitioner for a reputable medical company. This company has pioneered the manufacture of medicine for several life-threatening illnesses and through Miriam's endeavours, is riding on the crest of a wave. Its squeaky clean image has, up until now, never been tarnished. Then some shocking facts come to light.

One of the company's top researchers is caught selling harmful drugs. The police uncover a manufacturing plant in the company's basement where the researcher makes his potentially lethal pills, which he is allegedly selling to teenagers at raves.

The media headlines are shocking. All the newspapers carry the story of the researcher, the basement and the drugs.

The newspaper articles hint that the company is involved and that the staff had received a percentage of the sales. The researcher soon appears in court and pleads not guilty to several charges against him. He also implicates one of the staff members, Miriam's friend, in the scandal, saying that this person had helped him to produce and sell the drugs. The friend also appears in court.

What must Miriam do to save the company and help her friend who, she is certain, must be innocent? The directors of the company have instructed her to salvage the situation. Should Miriam keep quiet and issue no statements on behalf of the company and hope the nightmare will simply go away? Should she issue a statement in which she puts all the blame on the researcher and maintains that her friend is innocent? Should she try to deny police reports about the company's involvement? Should she explain to the media that the researcher has an extravagant lifestyle with a house, a luxury yacht and many overseas trips while her friend, who is supporting her sick mother and three brothers and sisters, is living a hand-to-mouth existence?

Questions

1. *If Miriam keeps completely quiet and issues no statements, what do you think will happen?*

2. *Should Miriam issue a statement saying that the company was unaware of what was going on and put the blame solely on the researcher? Support your answer by providing reasons.*

3. *Should Miriam issue a statement claiming that the whole incident has been blown out of proportion by the police and the media?*

4. *Should Miriam issue a statement explaining how the researcher probably sold drugs to maintain his extravagant lifestyle while her friend possibly helped him because of her much needier conditions at home?*

As a professional public relations practitioner, Miriam's first concern in dealing with this case has to be for the company for which she works. She has an obligation to try to protect her company's image and, in this case, it involves trying to repair the damage caused by the media, the police investigation and the court case.

Miriam must also bear in mind certain legal ethics. Firstly, if she tries to underplay the whole scenario, she could be undermining the police investigation. For example, if the police claim that drugs valued at hundreds of thousands of rand had been manufactured, while Miriam claims that they were of little value, who do you think the media will be likely to believe? In addition, Miriam, as well as the company she represents, will lose their credibility in the eyes of both the media and the public should the court case reveal that the police allegations had been correct, regardless of all the pioneering work that Miriam's company has done.

Issuing a news release blaming the researcher and proclaiming her friend's innocence is not a good course of action. Firstly, everyone, no matter who they are or what position they hold, is innocent until proven guilty. Secondly, Miriam's opinion regarding her friend's innocence is based on her personal involvement and is not objective. Besides, it is the court's task is to judge who is innocent and who is guilty.

Miriam should always remember that, once a person has appeared in court, the matter becomes *sub judice*, which means that no further statements about the case or about the people involved in the case can legally be made. In other words, should Miriam issue a statement describing the vastly different lives of the two accused, she would be acting contrary to the law. Miriam's best choice would be to be open with the press, to explain that the company was horrified by the police investigation and that it is giving the police its full co-operation. She could also mention that structures had been put in place to prevent a similar occurrence from happening in the future and that an internal investigation is under way at the company (if either of these statements is true). She should explain that she is not at liberty to say more about the case as the matter is now *sub judice* and should express her confidence in the process of the law.

Once the court has reached a verdict, she could issue a further statement expressing gratitude that the whole matter has now been dealt with. She should, under no circumstances, become involved with issuing statements about the private life of either of the accused or find excuses for any untoward behaviour.

 **Summary**

Legal ethics is much the same as moral ethics. In a case such as the one described here, the professional public relations practitioner must remain objective about the issues involved and must not pre-empt a court decision by giving out any information, no matter how trivial, while the hearing is in progress.

It is your duty, as public relations practitioner, to ensure that any statements you issue in such an instance are legally and ethically correct. In doing so, you and the company you work for remain credible. Overstep the mark and you lose all credibility.

Moral ethics, however, must not be considered to be irrelevant. In the course of a public relations practitioner's duties, the upholding of moral ethics is as important as the upholding of legal ethics. One small mistake on the part of Public Relations Practitioners can lead to numerous unforeseen problems that may even put his or her career in jeopardy. During your career you may be faced with many opportunities that may, at first, seem exciting and to your benefit. Beware, however, that failure on your part to uphold the Code of Professional Standards for the Practice of Public Relations may lead to nightmares instead of dreams. If you find yourself in a tricky situation and you are in doubt about any aspects of the code of conduct, consult a colleague or a professional. Never take a chance and think you will get away with it — eventually you will be found out.

 **Test yourself**

1. Explain the meaning of the terms 'moral ethics' and 'legal ethics', and give a practical example of each to support your answer. (Find your own examples — do not follow the examples given in this chapter.)

2. If you invite a journalist to lunch to strengthen professional relations, would you be acting against moral ethics? Support your answer by providing reasons.

3. In preparing your internal newsletter you come across an interesting article published in a magazine that you feel would be appropriate to publish in your newsletter. You copy this article word for word and neglect to give credit to the original magazine. Soon after your newsletter is published, the magazine takes legal action against both you, as editor, as well as the organisation. Explain the reason for this legal matter. What could you have done to prevent this?

Sources consulted

Newsom, D, Scott, A & Van Slyke, TJ (1993) *This is PR. The Realities of Public Relations*. California: Wadsworth.

Seitel, PF (1995) *The Practice of Public Relations*, New Jersey: Prentice Hall.

Willis, J & Willis, DB (1993) *New Directions in Media Management*, Massachusetts: Allyn & Bacon.

SENDING YOUR MESSAGE THROUGH THE MEDIA

One of the public relations practitioner's most important tasks is dealing with the media. When sending a message to the outside public, they have to consider various options. Their main channels are the various mass communication media that provide excellent potential for publicity.

Clever decisions on the part of the public relations practitioner could ultimately result in media coverage of a newsworthy incident, whereas a wrong approach could result in failure. Handling the media unprofessionally could result in negative publicity, which could cause an organisation immense harm. The power of the media should never be underestimated.

Understanding the media will not only result in effective and purposeful liaison between public relations practitioners and journalists. It will also enable public relations practitioners to decide when and for which media their message will be suitable. It further enables them to provide the type of effective information needed by each medium.

Dealing with the media is an ongoing process and regular contact with members of the different media should be maintained.

In this interactive relationship and in dealing with the public, it is important that journalists and public relations practitioners uphold certain ethical and social standards. The integrity of members of these two professions should never be in doubt. This would erode the trust of society and cause great damage to the image of both professions.

Introduction to the print media — newspapers and magazines

Objectives

After you have studied this chapter, you should be able to:

▶ describe what is meant by the print media;
▶ describe the nature of the print media;
▶ determine the advantages and disadvantages of the print media; and
▶ explain the importance of the readership and circulation of print media.

Introduction

Although the print and electronic media have the same aim, namely to inform, entertain and educate, they look and operate differently. Public relations practitioners should keep this important fact in mind when dealing with the media and should understand that certain obstacles may hamper or facilitate the end product generated by a specific medium.

In this chapter, we look at several general aspects of the print media. Although some might sound obvious, they can have an important influence on how public relations practitioners prepare and present their messages, as well as the way in which they deal with contact people in the different media.

The nature of the print media

In its broadest sense, the print media can be described as anything that is printed and distributed to the public. The print media comprise various publications, leaflets and pamphlets that can all be put to good use by public relations practitioners at some time for a specific purpose.

When dealing with the print media, there are certain important aspects to bear in mind. These include:

- different publications need information for different reasons (a daily newspaper mainly needs hard, factual news, whereas a specialised magazine such as *Car* needs information only on a specific subject);
- different publications have different target markets and public relations practitioners should acquaint themselves with these markets (*Business Day* focuses on businesspeople in general whereas *Fair Lady* focuses on women);
- readers (a publication's target market) determine, to a large extent, its content — they might also be the reason why an editor/subeditor will consider the public relations practitioner's story suitable or not;
- publications work to deadlines, therefore, it is no use sending information to a monthly magazine about something that will not be relevant at the time of publication — rather adapt the article by removing pieces imposing time limits;
- each publication has its own identity, created by using specific typefaces and fonts, colours, photographs and layout;
- good, top-quality photographs and graphics can add tremendously to a publication's appeal, but each publication has certain preferences in this regard. It is advisable to include people in photographs (where possible) and to 'tell a story' through creative photography;
- very few publications will use a news release in its original form. If one is used, it is rewritten according to the publication's style and to what the subeditor/journalist considers newsworthy. A publication may sometimes not be interested in a news release, but they may find something else in it — for example, a sentence or statement — worth following up. This does not mean they will definitely publish something, but it is possible that a completely different aspect, something you did not consider newsworthy, is covered.

Advantages and disadvantages of the print media

One of the most important characteristics of print media is that the reader must be literate and have the time and desire to read. Unlike the electronic media, which can be regulated by merely pushing a button, people who want to read have to put more effort into obtaining the publication, ie they have to buy or borrow it.

Once a publication has been obtained, the reader's attention is retained by eye-catching headlines, different fonts, typefaces, etc. Most importantly, the content must hold the reader's interest.

Print media are not restricted by time slots (as with the electronic media). Publications can be read anywhere at any time. Print media also have a longer lifespan than information transmitted through the electronic media.

Some differences between newspapers and magazines

When dealing with the different media, it is important that the public relations practitioner selects the right information and photographic material for different publications. The following aspects should be kept in mind:

Newspapers need accurate, factual information and photographs about newsworthy events immediately after the event has occurred. Photographs with news value are important. This is not the case with magazines, which have more time to work on a story. Magazines need good, top-quality photographs (they have the time to wait for them) and more background information in each article.

A magazine article need not have the news characteristics required by newspapers. Magazines use interesting, unique, human interest, educational or entertaining information for their articles.

Take note

Different publications publish different types of stories — and use different styles. Newspapers publish mainly:

▸ hard-news stories that are concise and written according to the 'inverted pyramid' style (Who, What, When, Where, Why, How — also known as 'the 5Ws + 1H'); and

▸ features, which are more detailed than hard-news stories.

Magazines, on the other hand, do not publish short, newspaperstyle stories, but use features, eg profiles, human interest features, light stories, etc.

Inverted pyramid:

Most important information to less important information

▸ The type of paper used by a publication will influence the end result. Photographs reproduced in a newspaper will not be of the same quality as those used in upmarket magazines because magazines are usually printed on a better-quality paper.

▸ Newspapers normally appear on a daily or weekly basis, whereas magazines mostly appear weekly, fortnightly or monthly. The public relations practitioner must keep this in mind and provide the right information at the right time. News for newspapers must be fresh, factual and of current value, whereas the same incident may be covered in more detail as an in-depth feature article in a magazine a few months later.

▸ Deadlines for newspapers must be kept daily (or weekly in the case of weekly newspapers), whereas deadlines for magazines can be set up to two months before the magazine is distributed.

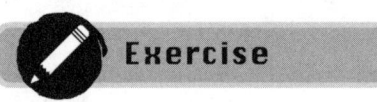

Exercise

Considering the differences between newspapers and magazines, compare a magazine to a daily newspaper with special reference to the differences in format, layout, fonts, quality of paper, types of article, etc. List the different articles appearing in each publication.

The print media in South Africa

Several large publishing groups in South Africa are responsible for most South African publications. They publish at least 27 urban, daily and weekly newspapers countrywide. These groups include *Naspers*, *Times Media*, *Perskor*, *New Africa Investments Limited (NAIL)* and others. Apart from these groups, there are also smaller companies and individuals who publish newspapers and magazines.

Major newspapers and magazines are linked to the Internet through the website *news24.com*, which provides news 24 hours a day, seven days a week, covering news, sports, business, etc.

> Find out which publications belong to which publishing group. This information can be found in every print medium. List the different publishing groups and the publications for which they are responsible.

Readership and circulation

Readership refers to the number of people who read newspapers and magazines (Jefkins 1992:51). Circulation figures indicate the average sales of each publication. When the circulation figure of a publication is compared with its readership, it will be found that the readership is higher than the circulation figure. Why? Let us look at the following example:

> *You buy a* YOU *magazine. You take it home and read it. Your spouse and three children also read the magazine. What has happened? One copy that was bought was read by five people! Therefore, the readership is higher than the circulation figure.*

Take note

It is important that the public relations practitioner knows where to find information on what is published in which areas, and which publication(s) are suitable for different purposes.

The estimated readership of publications, ie how many people read the publication once bought, the areas in which they are circulated and the number of copies normally sold are good guidelines. The Audit Bureau for Circulation (ABC) and the All Media Product Surveys (AMPS) publish this kind of information.

Putting the media to work

Most public relations practitioners know that a basic knowledge of the print media is merely a starting point. Personal and continuous contact with influential members of the media should be considered essential to a successful media relationship.

All public relations practitioners should have a list of publications that can be used, together with contact names and telephone/cellphone and fax numbers, as well as e-mail addresses. To make life easier, important points such as the type of information needed and the details of published articles relevant to the organisation should also be listed.

Summary

It is quite apparent that a basic knowledge of the print media will help the public relations practitioner eliminate unnecessary work when preparing information for possible publication. It will also guide the public relations practitioner in compiling different articles for different purposes in different publications.

The next two chapters deal with newspapers and magazines in more detail.

? Test yourself

1. List the most important differences between newspapers and magazines.

2. With reference to the nature of print media, discuss important aspects that public relations practitioners should bear in mind when they want to use print media to convey their message.

Sources consulted

Jefkins, F (1992) *Public Relations. M&E Business Handbooks*, London: Pitman.

Print media — newspapers

Objectives

After you have studied this chapter, you should be able to:

▶ discuss the physical appearance and style of newspapers;

▶ distinguish between different types of newspaper and illustrate how differences can be exploited by public relations practitioners;

▶ discuss the functions, content and target markets of newspapers;

▶ describe the structure of the editorial staff and their functions;

▶ identify the appropriate editorial staff members to contact with newsworthy information; and

▶ discuss how a newspaper journalist operates.

Introduction

The newspaper is one of the most important media through which public relations practitioners can send their messages to the outside public. It is, however, important to remember that the newsworthiness and nature of a news story will, to a large extent, determine its suitability for a specific newspaper. A newspaper's main aim is to give its readers the latest news and this determines what is published.

Although electronic media such as radio and television have eroded the power of the press and although the press has yet to adapt to the computer era and increasingly diverse electronic media, eg the Internet, the printed newspaper has, over many years, proved its importance as a conveyor of information.

To survive strong competition, the press has changed its image and goals over the years. It can now be considered the medium best able to supplement news broken by the electronic media by carrying additional background information. Newspapers now rely more on entertaining and educating their readers than they did in the past.

Although the press has an interesting history, we will not go into it here, but will focus on the importance of newspapers to the public relations practitioner. For this purpose, we need to know how newspapers are structured, how they operate and what they regard as important when gathering and writing news for their readers. We will look at local and national newspapers in South Africa to provide a basis from which new and prospective public relations practitioners, armed with knowledge of how the media operate, can establish good relationships with media people.

Types of newspapers

Newspapers are a part of our everyday life. They are sold on street corners and in shops, they are subscribed to or they are delivered free of charge to our homes as community newspapers. Posters with headlines are used to advertise a newspaper's main news of the day.

Apart from newspapers that are sold, there is a vast range of other, free ('knock-and-drop') newspapers. These newspapers are aimed mainly at local communities and, apart from their strong advertising complement, they contain important and interesting local community news.

Not all newspapers are available everywhere — some are confined to certain areas, and their names are often an indication of their distribution area. Think, for instance, of the *East Rand Herald* or the *Kagiso/Dobsonville Express*.

Newspapers are classified according to different criteria. These are:

- area of distribution;
- frequency of distribution; and
- paid-for/free newspapers.

Although the public relations practitioner should consider all these aspects, we will take a closer look at the area of distribution as one way of classifying newspapers. It might also help public relations practitioners to make a list of newspapers that will be of use in their specific area.

South Africa has 20 daily and 13 weekly newspapers, most in English. Some 14.5 million South Africans buy the urban dailies, while community newspapers have a circulation of 5.5 million.

There is also a range of general and specialised news websites which, in terms of the speed and breadth of their coverage, are on a par with the best in the world.

Apart from international newspapers, which are available in our bookstores, we find a number of South African daily newspapers such as the *Daily Sun*, *The Star*, *Sowetan*, *Beeld*, etc and weekly newspapers such as *The Sunday Times* and *Rapport*.

Information about daily and weekly newspapers is available online at: http://www.southafrica.infoless_info/sa_glance/constitution/971558.htm

National newspapers

These newspapers are distributed countrywide. They include daily newspapers such as *The Star* and the *Sowetan*, and weekly newspapers such as the *Sunday Times* and *Rapport*. National newspapers cover national and international issues, politics, crime and violence, economics, human interest stories, sport, etc. Coverage includes news of national interest, eg an increase in the petrol price, international investment in South Africa, a baby abducted from a hospital, etc.

Some national, daily newspapers allocate space for local news in certain areas on specific days of the week. News of various kinds will be suitable for supplements.

Regional newspapers

Regional newspapers are similar to national newspapers, except that they are distributed in certain regions only. These newspapers carry a variety of news reports and articles and are excellent media for the public relations practitioner. Regional newspapers include *Volksblad, Die Burger, Beeld* and *City Press*.

Local community newspapers

Local, community newspapers are usually published in tabloid format and their names usually indicate the community or area they serve, such as *Bloemnuus, The Roodepoort Record* and *Krugersdorp News*. These papers are very popular with their readers and most of them are delivered weekly and free of charge to all households in certain areas (hence the name 'knock-and-drop').

There are more than 400 local newspapers countrywide, of which a vast number belong to the Caxton group. Some of these newspapers cover a much wider area than local communities, towns or cities, especially in certain farming and more remote districts. Examples of these newspapers include *The Lowvelder*, the *District Mail* and the *Potchefstroom Herald*.

The cost of producing most community newspapers is largely covered by advertising aimed at the local market. Although advertisements might take up as much as 70% of available space, community newspapers remain popular with the markets they serve, as the available editorial space focuses on local-interest stories such as happenings at local schools, churches, organisations, communities, sports clubs, etc.

Community newspapers focus on the local community, concentrating on human-interest stories with few hard-news reports. Although the standard and coverage of the community newspaper cannot be compared to the daily newspaper, it plays a definite and important role for the public relations practitioner. These newspapers can often be used for articles which do not have a strong news angle, or which are only of interest to a certain community. Another factor favouring community newspapers is that they often give organisations editorial coverage when they buy advertising space. This gives the public relations practitioner an opportunity for further publicity that should be exploited.

It is important that the public relations practitioner has a fair knowledge of circulation and readership figures, as this will help ensure that the target market is reached through the relevant newspapers.

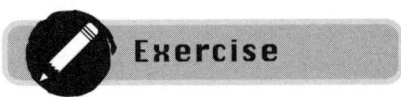

Exercise

Identify and list the various newspapers in your area that you can approach with newsworthy information.

The appearance and style of newpapers

Physical appearance

A newspaper is a relatively cheap publication containing the latest news and information on topical issues.

Newspapers differ in physical appearance. The two most popular sizes are the broadsheet (A2 size), such as *The Star, Business Day* and the *Sunday Times*, and the tabloid (pony) format (A3 size), such as the *Sowetan*, the *Citizen*, and most local and community newspapers.

The quality of paper on which newspapers are printed is of a relatively low grade as newspapers are not normally kept or stored. They have a shorter lifespan than, for example, magazines. News is gathered and published on a daily (or weekly) basis. Some daily newspapers have more than one edition. The edition is indicated on the front page by words such as 'late edition' or 'final edition'. The latest edition will have updates or fresh information on major stories.

Newspapers vary in volume and thickness. The space taken by advertisements often determines the newspaper's page count and space available for editorial matter. Advertising space is sold and takes up prominent positions on a page.

Style

Newspapers differ from one another because they are written, compiled and laid out according to their own style.

Take note

> '*Style*' *is a set of conventions governing the writing, language, punctuation and layout applied by staff members to a specific newspaper.*

Visual layout

Each newspaper strives towards a distinct appearance. Some newspapers prefer a sensational layout with large news photographs; big, bold headlines; and contrasting colours and sizes, whereas others may use a more conservative layout.

Compare, for instance, a front page of the *Sunday Times* with one of *Business Day*.

Balance, contrast, proportion and unity are important concepts to bear in mind when layout is done. This is discussed in chapter 16.

Legibility

The legibility of newspapers is important. Readers often spend limited time reading newspapers and they want to expend as little energy as possible in doing so. For this reason, newspapers use legible typefaces, short sentences and short reports. The language of any newspaper is simple and is aimed at as many readers as possible. Newspapers are written for a wide readership, from those with a Grade 9 (or equivalent) reading knowledge up to highly qualified readers.

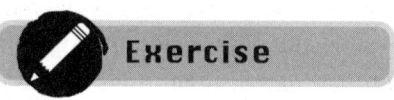

Exercise

Take any two newspapers, for example, the Sowetan *and* The Star, *and compare their physical appearance, their style, their visual layout and their legibility.*

	Sowetan	*The Star*
Physical appearance		
Style		
Visual layout		
Legibility		

Functions, target market and content

Functions

Newspapers play a very important role in our everyday lives and have certain distinct functions. Newspapers not only *inform* us of the latest news; they also *educate* and *entertain*. These functions are clearly illustrated by the hard news on the front page, the information on the entertainment pages and educational supplements.

Target market

Some newspapers are aimed at specific markets. *Business Day*, for example, is aimed at business and financial people. Other newspapers use supplements to cater for specific needs. A weekend supplement will appear before the weekend or a 'women's focus' supplement might be included on a certain day of the week.

Content

The content of a newspaper consists of more than news reports and features. Newspapers include regular columns, letters, cartoons, etc, which all play an important role in defining each paper's makeup. Newspapers provide what their readers want. The following graphic provides an interesting and useful picture illustrating how the standard content of a national newspaper may differ from that of a local community newspaper. This is merely an illustration, and newspapers might deviate from this norm. Local newspapers sometimes carry fewer *advertorials*. These differences indicate which newspapers could be used to publicise events.

Advertorial: editorial copy highlighting a product advertised on the same page

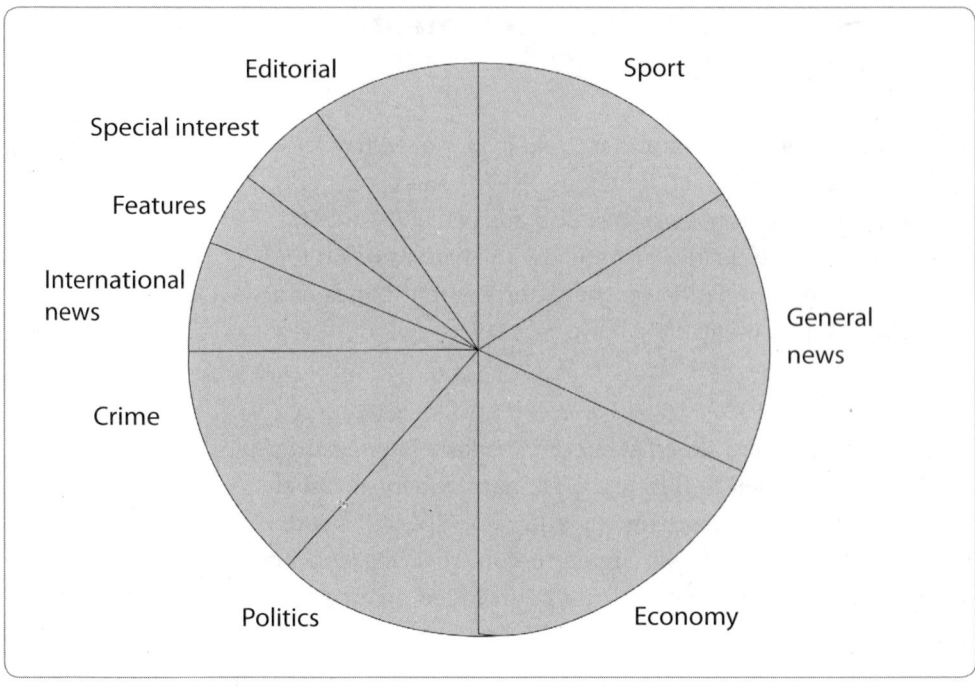

Figure 6.1A The content covered in a national newspaper

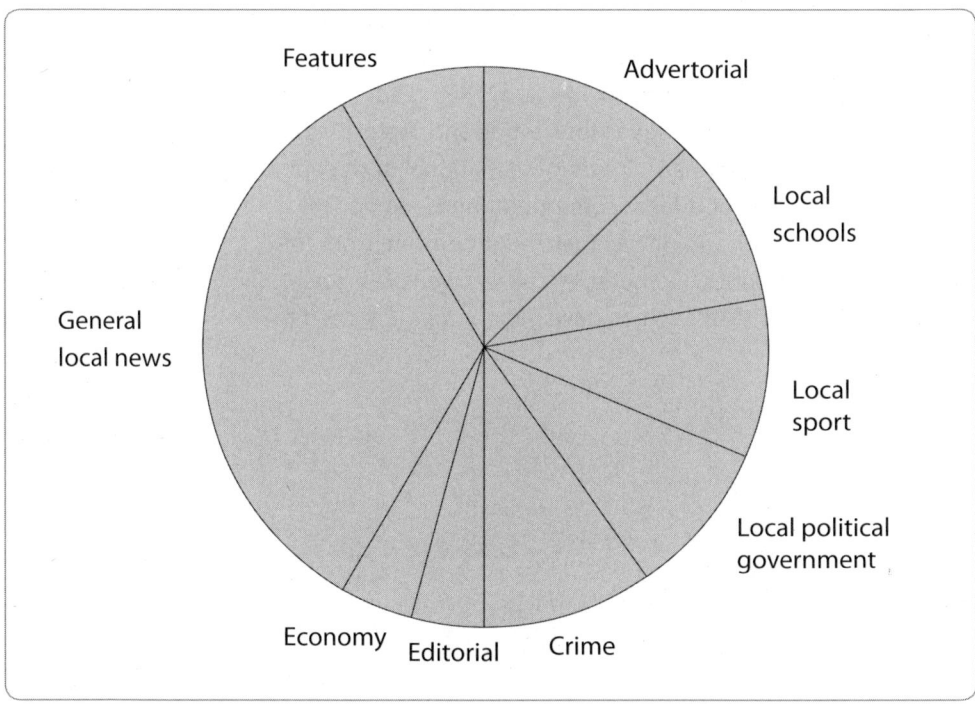

Figure 6.1B The content covered in local community newspapers

The content of a newspaper is normally organised or structured according to a standard layout. This means that certain types of news or articles are allocated to certain pages in a newspaper (such as sport on the back page) or even to certain columns (eg the editor's column on the upper left-hand side of the editorial/ leader page). The structure of each newspaper is also influenced by the newspaper's style and the image it wants to create.

Let us look at some of the standard pages found in a newspaper. (There may be more examples and their content may differ from these examples.)

Front page and other important news pages

The front page carries the most important news stories (headline news). A newspaper's name always appears in big bold letters on the front page in an area called the *masthead*. The front page 'sells' the newspaper and does not only have to be visually attractive but must also 'invite' the reader to buy the newspaper — by indicating what can be read inside. Apart from bold headlines for lead stories, so-called *teasers* are often used on a front page to indicate which stories can be read inside. (See more on the anatomy of the front page further on page 71.)

Masthead: a newspaper's name appears in big, bold letters on the front page

Teasers: focus on important/interesting stories inside the newspaper

The front page normally does not have more than four or five news reports (usually 'hard' news and one or two photographs). Other important news reports will be printed on pages 3 and 5 (odd right-hand pages), which are also considered important news pages. Any hard news on a company has a fairly good chance of appearing on these pages. Public relations practitioners must therefore always be prepared for and informed of any news event in their own organisation before speaking to the press. Unfortunately, it may often be negative news (a disaster, an emergency, crime, etc) that appears on these pages.

Editorial page

Editorial/leader page: page containing articles written by or on behalf of an editor giving opinions on topical issues

This page is usually an even-numbered page (page 2, 4, 6, etc) and has a standard layout. The *editorial (leader) page* is normally used for editorial and other comment. Newspapers strive to publish fair and objective news reports. The editorial page is used to comment on issues and/or news stories and reflects the opinion of the newspaper. In addition to the editor's comments, the rest of the page is used for other regular columns.

Women's page

The women's page, which is an important part of certain newspapers, provides for women's interests and for their needs and also ensures that women read newspapers. The type of information found on this page will include a variety of articles dedicated to the career woman, health care, child care and education, beauty, house and home, cooking, fashion, etc.

Financial page

Some newspapers have a large financial section that is not confined to one page, comprising a supplement (eg *Business Times*, a section of the *Sunday Times*). Although hard financial news stories will appear on one of the news pages, there are many other financial news stories that are considered to be important for readers. Financial news will include stock exchange news, bullion prices, political uncertainties, wars, financial investments, labour, economic developments, etc. Certain events, for example, the annual budget, can provide good financial stories that cannot all be adequately covered on the front page.

Entertainment/social page

The entertainment page gives information on the latest entertainment at theatres, cinemas, on television, etc. Popular restaurants might also feature on this page. The entertainment section can also be a supplement, especially at the end of the week, to publish information on entertainment taking place throughout the weekend.

Sports page

As South Africa is known for its interest in sport, there is enough sporting news to fill more than a page each day. Important sports stories might, however, be carried on the front pages — think of the many World Cup tournaments and international games in which South African sportspeople compete.

Anatomy of the front page

Reading a newspaper is easy if you know its different parts and what each contains, such as news, articles of opinion, features and advertisements. The front page of a newspaper needs to grab the most attention because readers are able to see the bold headline and any pictures which may affect the purchasing decision and it has a specific layout in terms of graphics, text and positioning. So what are the parts of the front page of a newspaper?

Some or all of these may be found on the front pages of newspapers:

- **Banner headline** — a headline that spans the full width of the page;
- **Block** — a picture;
- **Box-out** — a small part of the page, sometimes shaded in a different colour, to draw the reader's attention;
- **By-line** — the name of the reporter, which is often included at the beginning of the feature rather than at the end, or not at all;
- **Caption** — typed text under photographs explaining the image;
- **Credits** — mention of the author of a feature in the form of a by-line. Photographs may have the name of photographer or the agency that supplied them alongside them and reports may include the name of the news agency that sent them (eg SAPA, AP, Reuters);

- **Crosshead** — a subheading that appears in the body of the text and is centred above the column of text (if placed on to one side, it is called a **side-head**);
- **Cross-reference** — tells readers the headline of an article on another page that is connected with the story they have just read;
- **Dateline** — the place from where the report comes;
- **Ear** — an advertisement at the side of the masthead;
- **Edition logo** — used if a daily newspaper has several issues of the newspaper in print in one day, for example, the edition line identifies whether the newspaper publication is 'early', 'late', 'late final' and so on;
- **Exclusive** — coverage of a story by the newspaper and no one else, which may sometimes be paid for by the newspaper (eg a celebrity wedding);
- **Headline** — the main statement, usually in the largest and boldest font, describing the main story;
- **Kicker** — a story designed to stand out from the rest of the page by the use of a different font (typeface) and layout;
- **Lead story** — the main story on the front page, usually a splash;
- **Lure/teaser** — a word or phrase directing the reader to look inside the paper at a particular story or feature;
- **Masthead** — the title block or logo at the top of the front page identifying the newspaper, often set into a block of black or red/blue print or boxed with a border, plus the place of publication and date and sometimes containing an emblem or a motto;
- **Menu** — the list of contents inside the paper;
- **Nib** — stands for news-in-brief (a very short article);
- **Pugs** — the 'ears' of the page at the top left and right-hand corners of the paper, showing the price of the paper, the logo or a promotion that are well placed to catch the reader's eye;
- **Reverse blocks** — words in white on a dark background to stand out against the usual black-on-white headline;
- **Rule** — a heavy line;
- **Secondary lead** — usually only a picture and headline, which gives a sneak preview of a story that may be found inside the paper;
- **Sidebar** — when a main feature has an additional box or tinted panel along side of it;
- **Solus** — a solitary advertisement;

- **Splash** — the main story on the front of the paper, with the largest headline and a photograph;
- **Spread** — a story that covers more than one page;
- **Standfirst/lead paragraph** — an introductory paragraph before the start of the feature, sometimes in bold;
- **Strapline/subhead** — an introductory headline below the headline;
- **Tag** — a word or phrase used to engage a reader's interest in a story by categorising it, eg 'Exclusive' or 'Sensational'.

Let us study the 'front page' below and identify some its parts:

1. Ear/pug
2. Banner headline
3. Subhead/strapline
4. Solus
5. Masthead
6. Block

How many other parts can you identify?

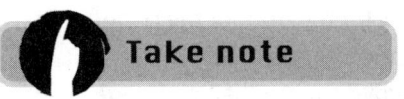

> Although this section on content focuses on newspapers, a similar layout can be adopted for in-house publications.

> Using the classification of newspapers' contents as a guideline, discuss how you, as a public relations practitioner, can apply a similar classification system to your in-house magazine.

Structure of editorial department and staff duties

Although newspapers differ as far as organisational structure is concerned, there are certain positions and duties that will always be peculiar to the press. A newspaper cannot function efficiently without an editorial department, an advertising department and a printing department. Let us look at the structure of the editorial department to get an idea of who is responsible for what at a newspaper. This will also give the public relations practitioner an idea of important contact people at the newspaper.

We look first at the standard editorial structure of a daily national newspaper and then at a local, community newspaper. The duties and responsibilities of each staff member are listed in brackets below their positions.

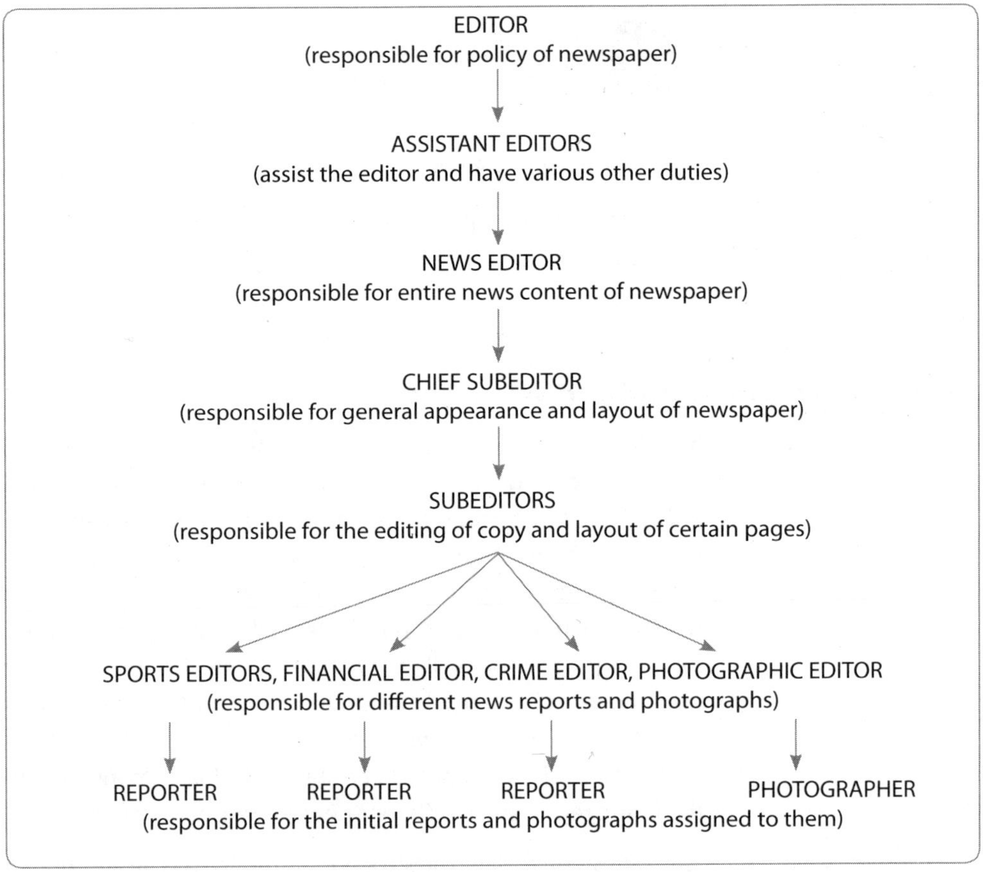

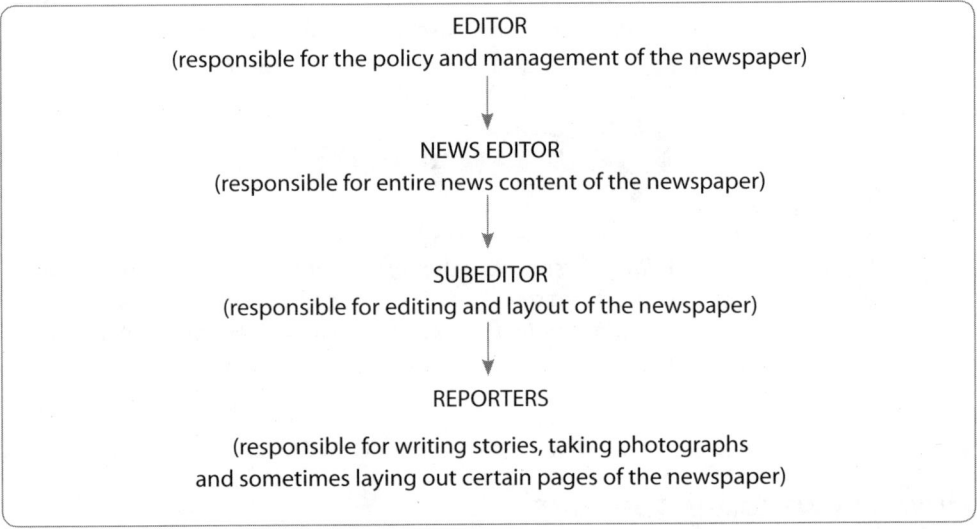

Figure 6.2 Editorial structure (daily national newspaper)

EDITOR
(responsible for policy of newspaper)

ASSISTANT EDITORS
(assist the editor and have various other duties)

NEWS EDITOR
(responsible for entire news content of newspaper)

CHIEF SUBEDITOR
(responsible for general appearance and layout of newspaper)

SUBEDITORS
(responsible for the editing of copy and layout of certain pages)

SPORTS EDITORS, FINANCIAL EDITOR, CRIME EDITOR, PHOTOGRAPHIC EDITOR
(responsible for different news reports and photographs)

REPORTER   REPORTER   REPORTER   PHOTOGRAPHER
(responsible for the initial reports and photographs assigned to them)

Figure 6.2 Editorial structure (daily national newspaper)

EDITOR
(responsible for the policy and management of the newspaper)

NEWS EDITOR
(responsible for entire news content of the newspaper)

SUBEDITOR
(responsible for editing and layout of the newspaper)

REPORTERS

(responsible for writing stories, taking photographs
and sometimes laying out certain pages of the newspaper)

Figure 6.3 Editorial structure (community newspaper)

Discuss the functions of the various editorial staff members of:

▶ a daily newspaper; and
▶ a community newspaper.

Whom to contact at the newspaper

It is important that the public relations practitioner knows whom to contact at the newspaper. Initial contact should always be made through the news editor, whose secretary will forward any information if he/she is not available and a reporter who covers a specific field (beat) will be assigned to the story. In many cases, this reporter will be the person a public relations practitioner will contact most often. A public relations practitioner at a financial bank will usually contact the financial reporters of different newspapers, whereas the public relations practitioner of a regional police station will have contact with the crime reporters of different newspapers in the area.

The editor of a daily newspaper normally has little contact with the public and is not the person the public relations practitioner should contact with a news story. This is, however, not necessarily the case with a local newspaper where the editor is often well known to the community.

With reference to your organisation, discuss who you will contact at a specific daily newspaper and at a local community newspaper when you want to convey newsworthy information to the public.

How a newspaper operates

News follows a certain route from the moment it is identified to when it is sold on the street corner as part of the newspaper.

In chapter 3, we discussed how news is identified. Let us look now at the rest of the process.

News stories are normally assigned to specific journalists by the news editor during a meeting. Journalists can also submit ideas of stories that they consider viable and may be instructed to write them. Once journalists have received their tasks for the day/week, they have to use every available source to gather as much information as possible for their news stories. They might have to work on more than one story at a time, and some will be more urgent than others. They might also be expected to take their own photographs or may have a photographer assigned to them. Once journalists have enough information, they will type it on a computer according to a standard format. The news editor normally tells reporters what is expected of them.

Reports must be completed to fit in with the newspaper's *deadline* and *press deadline*. Newspaper reports are normally written according to a structure in which the 'Who, What, When, Where, Why and How' questions are answered according to the inverted pyramid structure. This means that the report will start with the most important facts and end with the least important, or additional, facts. Paragraphs should be short and the first one should not exceed 26 words.

Deadline: the time by which copy should be submitted to the subeditor

Press deadline: the time at which a newspaper is handed to presses for printing

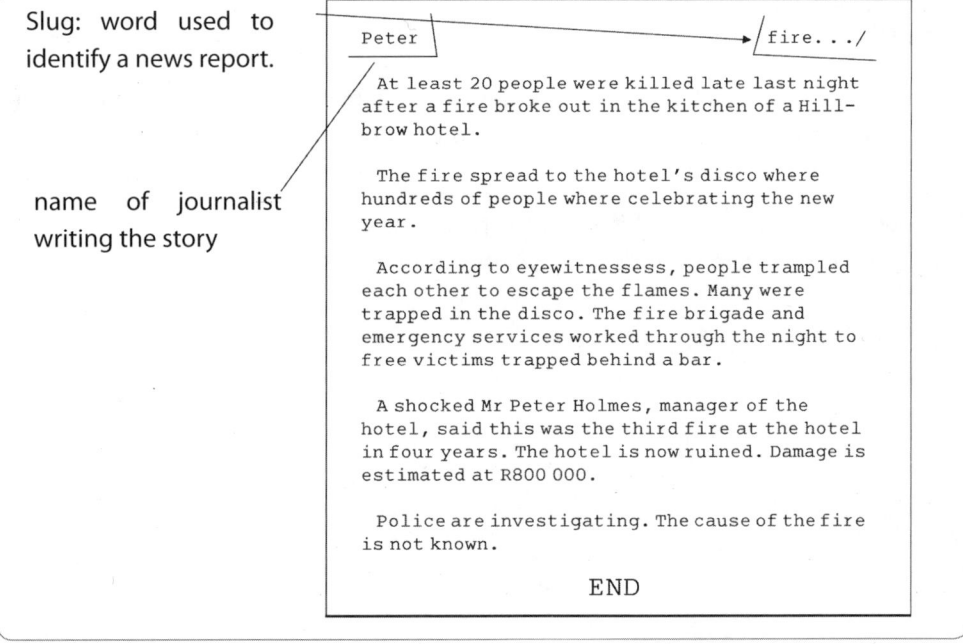

Slug: word used to identify a news report.

name of journalist writing the story

Peter ┐ ┌ fire.../

At least 20 people were killed late last night after a fire broke out in the kitchen of a Hill-brow hotel.

The fire spread to the hotel's disco where hundreds of people where celebrating the new year.

According to eyewitnessess, people trampled each other to escape the flames. Many were trapped in the disco. The fire brigade and emergency services worked through the night to free victims trapped behind a bar.

A shocked Mr Peter Holmes, manager of the hotel, said this was the third fire at the hotel in four years. The hotel is now ruined. Damage is estimated at R800 000.

Police are investigating. The cause of the fire is not known.

END

Figure 6.4   Example of a news report

Hard copy: news report printed on paper

This report is edited by the subeditor — usually on a computer or on the typed copy. If the subeditor edits on *hard copy*, he or she uses standard editing symbols. These are discussed in more detail in chapter 16.

Once stories have been checked by the subeditor, they are either sent back to the journalist to confirm or add facts or they are kept on the subeditor's desk for layout. Depending on the size of the newspaper, different categories of news stories are allocated to different pages and the reports are passed to the relevant subeditors for layout.

The stories used in each edition and the space afforded them depend on the stories' news value and the availability of space.

Stories are chosen for their newsworthiness. When the pages have been set and everybody concerned is satisfied with the result, the newspaper is sent to presses and then to the distributors.

At larger newspapers, the report goes through an even finer sifting process. The report firstly goes to the news editor on duty (ie night news editor), then to the editor on duty (ie night editor) who checks the facts and style before sending it to a subeditor to check the language and do the layout.

Summary

It is important to remember that, while this discussion gives detailed information about newspapers, public relations practitioners should know this information because they must:

- know whom to contact at different newspapers; and
- be able to use certain journalistic skills in their everyday work.

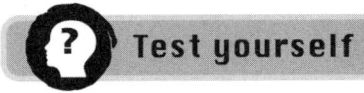
Test yourself

1. Discuss how newspapers differ from one another in their appearance, style and legibility.

2. Discuss the different types of newspaper.

3. What are the main functions of newspapers?

4. Discuss how newspapers organise their content and give a detailed description of the front page's content.

5. Discuss why it is important for the public relations practitioner to have a knowledge of the structure and functions of the editorial department and staff at newspapers.

6. Discuss the process a news story follows from the moment it is assigned to a specific journalist.

7. Study the front page of any newspaper and identify as many parts as you can. Provide labels for each part identified.

Sources consulted

Lieb, T (2009) *All the News: Writing and Reporting for Convergent Media*, Boston: Pearson Education.

The Press in South Africa. Available at: http://www.southafrica.info/ess_info/sa_glance/constitution/971558.htm [Accessed on: 24 March 2010]

Print media — magazines

Objectives

After you have studied this chapter, you should be able to:

▶ differentiate between categories of magazines; and

▶ describe the editorial structure of a magazine and the functions of each staff member.

Introduction

Public relations practitioners in the field would most probably agree that general magazines are not the best option when looking at the media as a means of sending a message to the outside public. Should public relations practitioners consider magazines, they should think carefully about their message and concentrate on specialised magazines.

We will, however, look at the different magazines on the market and the way in which they operate, as this will broaden your knowledge of magazines.

Please note that this chapter does not include internal and external house magazines, but focuses on those that are not linked to the organisation and form part of the general print media.

What makes a publication a magazine?

Magazines have various characteristics distinguishing them from other publications. They are colourful and are normally printed in an A4 format on good-quality paper. They appear weekly, fortnightly or monthly, are relatively expensive, rather thick and contain lots of information covering almost anything under the sun. Magazines use lots of photographs and carry a high percentage of advertisements.

Because of their high production cost, magazines are normally sold at various points of sale and not, as in the case of some newspapers, distributed free of charge. They can also be subscribed to.

Types of magazines

As in the case of newspapers, it is no easy task to classify South African magazines according to definite categories. There are a few existing classifications (De Beer 1993:110–117; Skinner, Von Essen & Mersham 2007) which we will examine below. These are not the only categories. There is scope for other, smaller categories.

Let us look briefly at examples of magazines in each of the following categories. They are almost self-explanatory and we will not discuss them in much detail.

Family magazines

Family magazines contain a variety of articles suitable for the whole family. This category includes magazines such as *YOU*, *Huisgenoot*, *Your Family*, *Bona* and *Drum*.

Women's magazines

Magazines focusing on women including *Fair Lady*, *Rooi Rose*, *Sarie*, *Living & Loving*, *Destiny woman*, *Essentials*, *Lééf*, *Psychologies* and *Vrouekeur*. The content of these magazines includes articles on fashion, skin care, food, health, diet, careers, etc.

Youth magazines

These magazines are aimed at teenage and young adult readers, and include publications such as *Talk* and *Young Time*.

These days self-explanatory subdivisions of youth magazines include categories for teens, with magazine such as *Seventeen* and *Saltwater Girl*, as well as categories aimed at *children*, with magazines such as *National Geographic Kids*.

Financial magazines

Magazines in this category are for business and financial people, and include publications such as *Financial Mail*, *Finansies en Tegniek*, *Finance Week*, etc.

Farming, agricultural and wildlife magazines

These magazines cover a wide range of subjects as South Africa is known not only for farming, but also for its wildlife. Magazines in this category include *Farmers Weekly*, *Landbou Weekblad*, *Effective Farming/Effektiewe Boerdery*, *African Wildlife*, etc.

Professional magazines

Professional magazines are aimed at specific, professional sectors of the reading market. They are characterised by a strong professional and scientific approach and are also referred to as 'association-linked' or 'society-linked' magazines. Examples are *Architecture SA*, *The SA Journal for Journalists*, *Suid-Afrikaanse Tydskrif vir Ekonomie*, etc.

Business and trade magazines

As this category indicates, these magazines include information on business, trade and industry. Some examples in this category are *Computing SA*, *South African Computer Buyer*, *Engineering News* and *Medicine Today*.

Special-interest magazines

There use to be several special-interest magazines that covered miscellaneous subjects and did not fit a specific category. However, many more categories have emerged (see http://www.magazines.co.za/home.html), such as:

- **Sports:** *Sports Illustrated, Golf Digest, Complete Golfer;*
- **Animals and pets:** *SA Horseman;*
- **Bridal and weddings:** *Bruid, Konfetti, Bridal Magazine;*
- **Entertainment:** *People;*
- **Estate living:** *Status quo;*

- **Fashion and style:** *Elle, Cleo, Glossy;*
- **Food and lifestyle:** *Avocado;*
- **Food and home:** *Sarie Kos, Wine;*
- **Health and fitness:** *Shape, Men's Health;*
- **Homes and gardens:** *Garden and Home, SA Garden, SA Tuin Paleis, SA Home Owner, The Gardener, Elle Decoration, Tuis, Home;*
- **Lifestyle:** *Simply Green, Vision, South;*
- **Men:** *Destiny Man;*
- **Motoring:** *Car, Wheels, Wiel;*
- **Parenting:** *Living & Loving;*
- **Science and technology:** *Popular Mechanics, Stuff;*
- **Travel and leisure:** *Country Life, Getaway, Retreat, Weg.*

 **Exercise**

Take any two magazines and list five articles in each magazine. See if you can link the article to a certain organisation/ company, which may have been responsible for some of the information in each article.

Magazine 1:

ARTICLE	ORGANISATION/COMPANY

Magazine 2:

ARTICLE	ORGANISATION/COMPANY

Functions, readers and content

Although the main *functions* of newspapers (to inform, educate and entertain) also apply to magazines, there are major differences in the priorities allocated to these functions. Most magazines rely heavily on providing light reading matter of an entertaining nature. At the same time, they keep readers up to date with the latest information in various fields.

Considering the variety of magazines, it is not difficult to see that magazines are directed at certain *markets*. Although there are many magazines for specialist groups, eg financiers and professional people, most magazines cater for a large readership and include articles on a variety of subjects.

The *content and layout* of many magazines follow standard formulae. A magazine's table of contents, usually on the second or third page, lists its articles and columns. Certain standard pages are found in every edition, eg front pages, editorial pages, etc. These pages normally follow the same sequence in every edition with regular articles/columns. The content of a typical women's magazine will include letters to the editor, fashion, cookery, short stories, etc, in the same sequence in most editions.

 **Exercise**

Take three different editions of your favorite magazine and write down the table of contents of each. Compare these and write down which ones can be considered as standard sections that appear regularly. Also, make a list of the articles categorised under each section.

Editorial structure and functions of each member

Magazines normally use freelance writers and photographers and research all possible sources for interesting articles. Much research goes into certain ideas to create or find a fresh, innovative angle. Standard news releases sent to magazines are often rewritten and published if they provide scope for another angle to be exploited. The permanent staff of magazines is trimmed to fill only the most important positions.

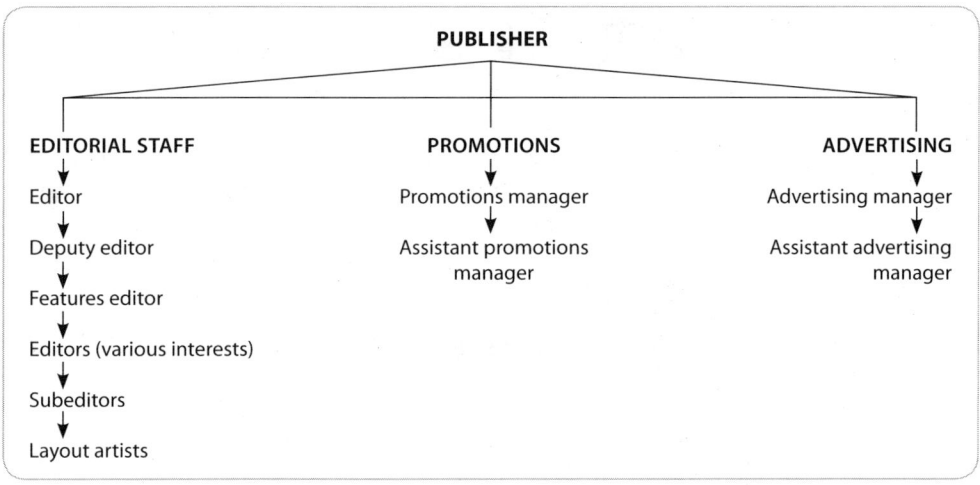

Figure 7.1 Organogram of a typical magazine

Functions of members of staff

Editorial staff

Each staff member's duties are clearly set out. The editor's role differs from that of a newspaper editor in that a magazine editor decides the publication's content. He/she will suggest ideas or topics that have to be followed up by the editor responsible for material in that specific field. Each editor, eg features editor, art editor, etc is responsible for editing articles for a specific section and liaising with the editor on the final product.

Promotions

Promotions are an important part of magazine publishing and are free publicity opportunities that provide added value for readers. A promotion could entail a competition offering sponsored prizes, eg an overseas trip sponsored by a travel agent. Staff in this section is responsible for writing promotional articles.

Advertising section

Staff of the advertising section of a magazine is responsible for selling advertising space. This section is of particular importance as income from advertising is used to cover part of the magazine's production costs.

Magazines are expensive publications. Although they are paid for by readers, their production costs cannot be covered if they do not sell advertising space.

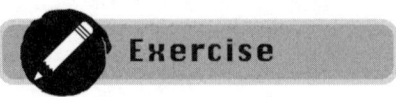

Using your own organisation:

▶ *Write a suitable article for a specific magazine about something new/unique in your organisation.*

▶ *Design and write a promotions article offering a prize.*

How magazines operate

Magazines operate slightly differently to newspapers for many different reasons.

Feature articles: articles that do not necessarily contain news, but give background information, comment, opinion, etc. Feature articles are suitable for magazines

More preparation and planning are needed to fill a magazine than for a newspaper. A magazine's *feature articles* are longer and need more research than those that appear in newspapers. Although magazines also work to deadlines, they do not experience the same rush as daily newspapers because they are published weekly, fortnightly or monthly.

Meetings are held to discuss the content of each edition. These meetings serve two purposes. They are held to determine the material available for the next issue and new possibilities, material and requests are discussed. The editorial staff works as a team to fill each edition with quality material.

The editor should receive copy at least six to eight weeks before publication. Once a topic has been researched and the story written and approved by the editor, it goes to the subeditor for subediting, the writing of headlines and, if necessary, a 'blurb' or information block. A blurb summarises an article or photographic page and is printed in a box near the headline. It gives a brief explanation of the article/photographic page.

From the subeditor, the article goes to the studio for layout, which is normally done on computer. It is then sent back to the subeditor for copy editing.

A publication must be 'print ready' and reach the printers at least two weeks before publication.

The public relations practitioner and magazines

Apart from specialised magazines which, in many cases, are the better option for public relations efforts, promotional articles in general magazines are another way of obtaining publicity for an organisation. Careful planning and thorough research are important. Magazine journalists and photographers should also be invited to social functions or important organisational events. However, the event should be unique, guests should include popular celebrities or public personalities and the occasion must offer possibilities for interesting articles.

Personal contact with magazine personnel is important. For example, a public relations practitioner working for a dairy or health product company should establish contact and a build relationship with a magazine's food or cookery editor. The public relations practitioner can then send regular news releases or stories to that editor.

If the public relations practitioner does not know anybody at the magazine, he/she should send a news release to the editor. Clear, appropriate photographs, contact persons and suggested angles for a story can turn a news release into an interesting article.

Submission dates and the frequency of publication are important, as they will determine whether your information is on time and relevant to the publication.

Take note

> *Public relations practitioners often have to comment on controversial matters. For example, a pharmaceutical product that caused the death of a patient is the subject of an investigative article and you, as a public relations practitioner, are contacted by a journalist who questions you on the use of the product in your hospital. In such a case, you need to be well informed or must ensure that your hospital's spokesperson is competent.*

Summary

Although the possibility of using magazines may appear remote for some organisations, it is still worthwhile to research their content and relevance as the opportunity to use them may arise unexpectedly.

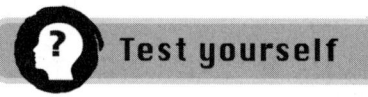

Test yourself

1. List the characteristics of a magazine.

2. List the different types of magazine and give examples of each.

3. What do you understand by the term 'promotions'?

4. Explain the difference between promotions and advertisements.

5. Explain the role external magazines can play in public relations.

Sources consulted

De Beer, AS (1993) *Mass Media for the Nineties — The South African Handbook of Mass Communication*, Pretoria: JL van Schaik (Pty) Ltd.

Skinner, JC, Von Essen, LM & Mersham, G (2007) *Handbook of Public Relations* (8 ed), Cape Town: Oxford.

Introduction to the electronic media — television and radio

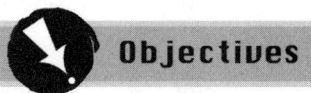

Objectives

After you have studied this chapter, you should be able to:

▶ discuss the television network of the SABC; and

▶ discuss the radio network of the SABC.

Introduction

In South Africa, most of the major cities have access to satellite communication. Radio has a 94% reach while that of television is 84% (Duncan 2009:43). Although technology has advanced at a rapid rate across the world, in South Africa there are stark disparities in terms of access to the electronic media (eg the Internet). This means that access to information is different across the country. Based on this, it is important for the public relations practitioner to be knowledgeable and have an understanding of the various electronic media. This will ensure that the electronic media can be used to convey important newsworthy information to the target audience according to accessibility. This is important because in most cases, public relations practitioners need to demonstrate the value of managed communication and its impact on a return on investment (ROI).

Because the South African Broadcasting Corporation (SABC) offers several national and regionally based television and radio services, this chapter is an introduction to the electronic mass-communication media emphasising the role played by the SABC. Public relations practitioners should, however, also consider using the services of the many community radio stations owned by private broadcasters.

The South African Broadcasting Corporation

The South African Broadcasting Corporation (SABC) is a public broadcaster and the services it offers can be used by public relations practitioners to reach a wide and diverse audience. The SABC's main functions are to disseminate information and provide viewers with educational and entertaining programmes.

The public relations practitioner's main involvement in the electronic media will be influenced predominantly by the public broadcaster's information dissemination function. Public relations activities can and do relate to the SABC's educational and entertainment functions, but we will focus on its information dissemination. We do so because the public relations practitioner's function is primarily geared to the dissemination of newsworthy information to the news and news-related departments of radio and television.

The reconstruction and development of South Africa demand that the SABC undergo many changes. The SABC has embarked on major restructuring and now operates according to business principles as it meets the challenge of thriving in an increasingly competitive broadcasting environment.

The SABC's head office at Broadcasting Centre in Johannesburg is one of the most modern complexes of its kind in the world, consisting of a 36-storey administration building and vast television and radio studio facilities.

The SABC has smaller broadcasting operations in all South Africa's main centres and offices and studios in several towns and cities. It has permanent offices in London, England.

The SABC board

All governance in the SABC is ultimately under the auspices of the organisation's board. The board is constituted and operates in accordance with the Broadcasting Act, as well as within the structures dictated by the Corporation's Memorandum and Articles of Association, the Board Charter and the Shareholder Compact. The SABC has a unitary board structure comprising 12 independent non-executive directors and three executive directors. The non-executive directors are nominated by the public and appointed by the President of the Republic of South Africa on the recommendation of parliament's Portfolio Committee on Communications. The executive directors are appointed by the board in consultation with the shareholders for a period not exceeding five years at a time. The three executive directors are the group chief executive officer, the chief operations officer and the chief financial officer (SABC Annual Report 2008/2009: 85).

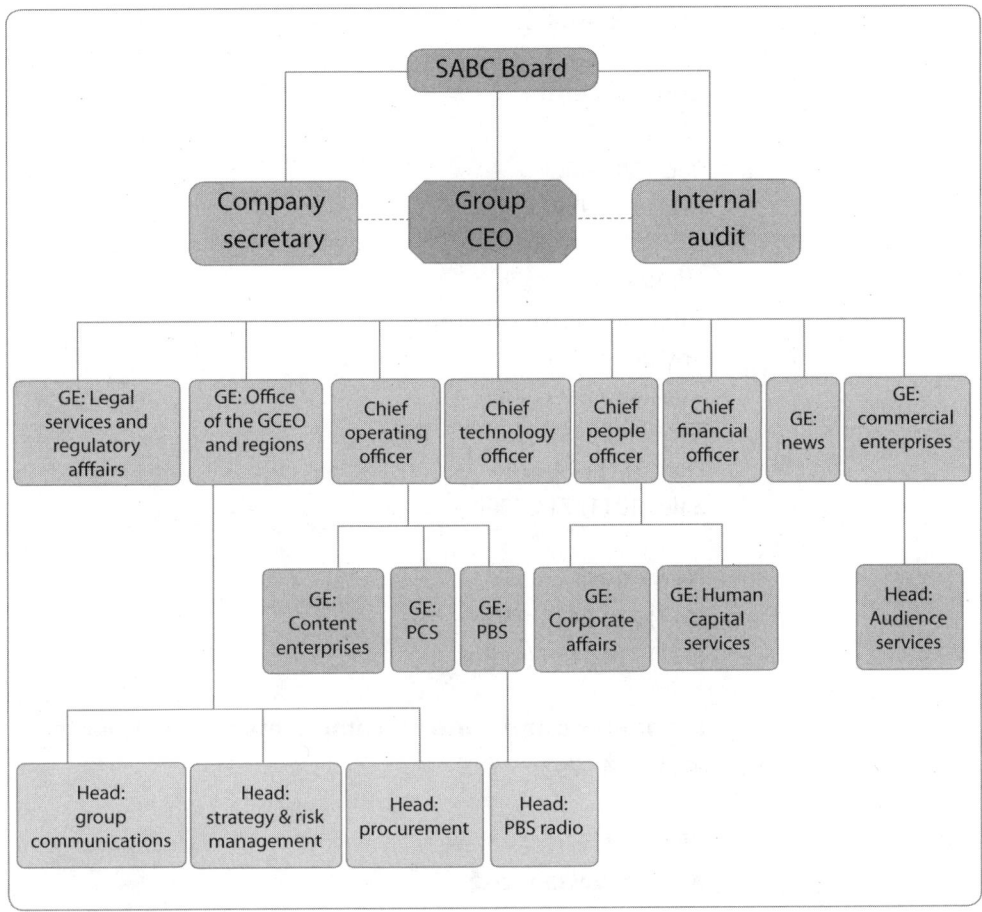

Figure 8.1 The SABC's organisational structure: SABC Annual Report 2008/2009

SABC news contact details

The SABC established its own website to reach a wider audience. With a rapidly changing news environment, the SABC took the decision to be a leader in the new marketplace. The decision was also based on the requirements to inform the public. The SABC is also in the unique position to supply a broad range of news that include both audio and video bulletins.

The main source of information for the sabcnews.com website is its own vast pool of reporters. The website will tap information gathered by reporters and radio and television current affairs programmes.

The SABC call centre is the link between the public and the SABC. To inform the SABC of a news story, one can send an e-mail to Feedback@sabcnews.com or call the contact centre.

Contact centre
086 100 7222
086 100 SABC
(011) 714 9797

Head office
Johannesburg (Gauteng)
Private Bag X1
Auckland Park, 2006
Tel: (011) 714 9111
Fax: (011) 714 9744
Sales: (011) 714 7000

News desk
(011) 714 2433 (TV)
(011) 714 5434 (radio)

Programme and editorial complaints and comments
(011) 714 9797

Website
http://www.sabc.co.za

The television network

South Africa has the largest television audience in Africa (South Africa online 2010) with more than four million licensed television households. The SABC's television network comprises three full-spectrum free-to-air channels and one satellite pay-TV channel aimed at audiences across the African continent. Combined, the free-to-air channels attract more than 17 million adult viewers per day. The three channels are SABC1, SABC2 and SABC3.

The one satellite pay-TV channel is SABC Africa. SABC1, 2 and 3 are called free-to-air channels because one does not need to pay a monthly subscription fee to watch them. Along with e.tv, these are the only free–to air–channels in the country.

Let us take a closer look at the SABC television channels:

SABC1

With more than 15 million viewers per week, SABC1 is the number one channel in the country. The channel projects a youthful brand image and quality but this is not to be confused with who watches it. In the same way that Coca-Cola is a youthful brand with a broad range of consumers, SABC1 aims to build a consistent brand quality while remaining a mass-volume channel reaching the most television viewers on any day. The channel boasts a monthly cumulative audience reach (a measure of the total number of unique listeners/viewers over a certain period) of 86%, according to the South African Advertising Research Foundation (SAARF 2010).

The channel views its audience as intelligent media-savvy citizens. While they face huge challenges in life, they are optimistic about the future of South Africa. They have an appetite for a broad range of programmes — from the escapism of the soaps and movies to information like news and current affairs, as well as educational programmes.

SABC2

SABC2 is a South African family-orientated channel with a nation-building focus and aspirations to create shared experiences, particularly around events of national importance. The channel also aims to help South Africans understand their relationship with their neighbours and their roles as citizens of South Africa and to find a sense of common identity as South Africans.

The channel caters for five distinct language groups (seSotho, Afrikaans, XITsonga, Tshi Venda and English).

Approximately 52% of SABC2 viewers fall into the 35-and-over age group. Of the viewers, 48% are English– and Afrikaans speaking while 52% are Nguni– and Sotho speaking. The channel has a monthly cumulative audience reach of 83% (SAARF 2010).

SABC3

SABC3 is a full-spectrum channel delivering everything an English-speaking or -understanding South African wants from television — all on one channel. The channel delivers entertainment, information and insight to upmarket South Africans, mostly urban, achievers with a world view.

English is the predominant language of broadcast on the channel although there have been attempts to increase multilingualism. Approximately 28.8% of the viewers are English speaking, 23.9% Afrikaans speaking, 23.4% Nguni speaking and 22.9% Sotho speaking. The channel has a monthly cumulative audience reach of 80% (SAARF 2010). It is interesting to note — especially for public relations practitioners — that the SABC's channels offer 24-hour programming which, in a year of broadcasting, amounts to more than 2 000 hours of news and news-related programmes; more than 800 hours of magazine and documentary programmes; more than 1 000 hours of educational programmes; and almost 100 hours of programmes dealing directly with the ecology. Many hours are also spent on feature films, serials, series, single dramas and situation comedies (sitcoms), youth and children's programmes, sport, variety, music, as well as formal and informal religious programmes.

Central to their focus on the information function, ie the information dissemination function of television news, it is interesting to note that in 1996, 98 news bulletins were broadcast each week. Television news is fed to the SABC by news teams gathering newsworthy items countrywide. These items are then broadcast in news bulletins and news-related programmes. Domestic contributions are supplemented by international news beamed to the SABC by satellite from international news agencies.

We take a closer look at the television newsroom's functions and the television journalist's duties in chapter 9.

The radio network

Radio continues to grow at national, regional and local levels, taking advantage of the new platforms of satellite, digital transmission and the Internet. One is able to listen to radio on the airwaves, via satellite and on the Internet. Some of the main radio stations offer live audio streaming from their websites. After South Africa became a democracy in 1994, a greater choice of stations and programming became available.

The SABC used to be the only institution with a licence to broadcast radio services. In 1996, some of the SABC's regional (commercial) radio services, including Highveld Stereo, Radio Jacaranda, Radio Oranje (now OFM), KFM, East Coast Radio and Radio Algoa were sold to private broadcasters.

Such changes affect public relations practitioners. It is important that they inform themselves of these and other changes, especially as independent radio services increase and grow. The number of community radio stations is also increasing. Smaller areas, ie cities and towns, are the focus of these radio services. Public relations practitioners can use these services to great advantage.

Important for public relations is that 12% of the radio schedule is devoted to news and news-related programmes. Copy supplied to radio news departments from various sources is compiled 24 hours a day into more than 150 news bulletins broadcast over SABC radio daily. Actuality programmes, talk shows, magazine programmes and documentaries comprise 20% of the radio schedule. Many hours are also devoted to programmes covering music, drama, religion, education, sport, the environment, conservation and other subjects.

About 30 editorial offices, a countrywide network of approximately 1 300 correspondents, more than 2 000 news contacts and the South African Press Association (SAPA) gather information for local news programmes. World news is provided by six international news agencies, 20 strategically situated foreign correspondents and a news-monitoring section.

News items are analysed and put into context to clarify them and lend perspective. The news division uses a computer system that is one of the most advanced in the world.

Chapter 10 deals with the structure and functions of the radio newsroom and elaborates on how radio journalists work.

All 11 of South Africa's official languages receive radio airtime and fall into three broad categories: public broadcast stations, commercial radio stations and community radio stations.

Public broadcast stations

- Lesedi FM
- Lotus FM
- Radio Sonder Grense
- SAfm
- Ukhozi FM
- Umhlobo Wenene FM

Public service radio

As the country's public service broadcaster, the SABC, while wholly owned by the state, is financially independent of taxpayers' money, deriving its income from advertising and licence fees in a ratio of four to one.

The SABC's mandate is to provide both a commercial and a public service, each administered separately, with commercial radio stations subsidising the public service stations. The corporation's commercial stations include 5FM, a national youth music station; Metro FM, a music station targeting black urban youth; and Channel Africa, an external radio service broadcasting in a number of languages across the continent.

The corporation's public broadcasting arm includes cultural services in all 11 official languages, as well as stations for South Africa's Indian (Lotus FM) and San (X-K FM) communities. By far the largest radio station in South Africa is Ukhozi FM, the SABC's isiZulu cultural service, with 6.38 million listeners per week.

Commercial radio stations

During the apartheid era, South Africa had only two independent radio stations: Radio 702 and Capital Radio. With the deregulation and liberalisation of broadcasting in the late 1990s, the number of commercial stations operating outside of SABC control proliferated.

In 1996, six lucrative SABC stations were privatised: Gauteng's Highveld Stereo and Radio Jacaranda, KwaZulu-Natal's East Coast

Radio, the Western Cape's KFM, the Eastern Cape's Radio Algoa and the Free State's OFM. The government raised over R500 million as the stations were licensed to various Black Economic Empowerment (BEE) groups.

In early 1997, eight new commercial radio licences were granted for broadcasting in South Africa's three biggest cities — Johannesburg, Cape Town and Durban.

Applicants targeting black audiences with new formats were generally favoured with two smooth jazz licences, P4 in Cape Town and Durban; one kwaito station, YFM; and one urban contemporary station, Kaya FM. The remaining four licences went to an English-language talk station, Cape Talk; two Afrikaans talk stations, Punt in Cape Town and Durban; and a classical music station, Classic FM.

- 5FM
- 702 Talk Radio
- Algoa FM
- Cape Talk
- Channel Africa
- Classic FM
- East Coast Radio
- Good Hope FM
- Highveld Stereo
- Jacaranda FM
- Kaya FM
- Kfm
- Metro FM
- M Power FM
- OFM
- Yfm

Radio frequencies

THE POWER OF 5FM	JHB-98.0 FM DBN-89.9FM BFT-91.3FM CPT-89.9FM	lotus fm	PE-98.3FM GP-106.8FM CPT-97.8FM KZN-87.7FM	ukhozi	90.8-107.4FM
METRO FM	JHB-96.4FM BFT-98.1FM WESTERN CAPE-88.6FM EASTERN CAPE-107.7FM DBN-93.0FM PTR-92.4FM MIDDELBURG-100.3FM	M	87.9-107.9FM	uhlobo lenene	88-106FM
			88.2-107FM	X-K	107.9FM
		RADIO 2000	98-102FM	ML	89.4-103.2FM
1000 HOT	94-97FM	RSG	100-104FM		
iKwezi	91.8-107FM	SAfm	104-107FM		
LESEDI FM	87.7-106.6FM	THOBELA	87.6-92.1FM		
Motsweding	87.7-104.0FM	tru fm	EASTERN CAPE-89.9-104.1FM		

Figure 8.2 Frequencies for all SABC radio stations in the regions (SABC Annual Report 2008/2009:106)

Community radio stations

- 906 FM Vaal Radio
- Bay FM
- Bush Radio
- Campus Radio
- CCFM
- Fine Music Radio
- Highway Radio
- Hindvani FM
- Impact Radio Kingfisher FM
- Link FM
- Overvaal Stereo
- Radio 786
- Radio Helderberg
- Radio Islam
- Radio Khwezi
- Radio Kragbron
- Radio Laeveld
- Radio Panorama
- Radio Pretoria
- Radio Pulpit/ Radio Kansel
- Radio Rippel
- Radio Riverside
- Radio Rosestad
- Rhodes Music Radio
- Tuks FM
- UCT Radio
- Voice of the Cape

From 1994 onwards, South Africa's broadcasting authority processed hundreds of community radio licence applications from groups as diverse as rural women's co-operatives, Afrikaans communities and various religious bodies.

The country now has over 100 community stations, broadcasting in many different languages. Their scope and reach varies enormously — from the half-a-million Jo'burgers who make up the audience of Jozi FM to, for example, the mere 1 000 people who listen to Ilitha Community Radio in the Eastern Cape town of Maclear.

Although community radio, by its nature, struggles to access advertising and other forms of financing, it is a crucial part of the South African broadcasting landscape, providing diversity for listeners and much-needed skills for the commercial radio sector.

Regulating the industry

Broadcasting in South Africa is regulated by the Independent Communications Authority of South Africa (Icasa), which issues broadcast licences; ensures universal service and access; monitors the industry and enforces compliance with rules, regulations and policies; hears disputes brought by industry or members of the public against licensees; plans, controls and manages the frequency spectrum; and protects consumers from unfair business practices (South Africa.info).

General

The SABC's Group Communication Department at the Johannesburg headquarters arranges visits to the broadcasting centre. To learn more about the activities of radio and television, it is advisable to arrange such a visit. To visit broadcast centres in other areas, the relevant general manager should be contacted.

The SABC's Group Publications Directorate also publishes a booklet, *Who's Where at the SABC*, which is worthwhile obtaining as it will help the public relations practitioner identify contact personnel at the SABC and gives further details on the SABC's organisational structure.

Summary

This chapter reflects the complexity of the electronic media. The SABC renders an essential service to a vast array of different target markets. The radio and television networks both broadcast in 11 languages.

The main functions of the electronic media are to inform, educate and entertain. The information function is the one most relevant to public relations practitioners, as they should focus on programmes relevant to the dissemination of information. This function is located in the news and news-related programmes offered by the television and radio networks.

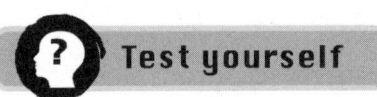

Test yourself

1. Discuss the SABC's television and radio networks.

2. Why is it important for public relations practitioners to align themselves with the public broadcaster's information dissemination function?

Sources consulted

Duncan, J (2009) *South Africa — Migration Underway*. In Berger, G (ed) *Beyond Broadcasting: The Future of State-owned Broadcasters in Southern Africa*, Grahamstown: Highway Africa, 43–54.

SABC Annual Report 2008/2009

South Africa.info. Available at: http://www.southafrica.info/about/media/radio.htm [Accessed on: 23 February 2010].

South Africa online (2010) *Communications*. Available at: http://www.southafrica.co.za/about-south-africa/science-and-technology/communications/ [Accessed on: 3 September 2010].

South African Advertising Research Foundation (SAARF) (2010) *Television Audience Media Survey*, Available at: http://www.saarf.co.za/ [Accessed on: 3 September 2010].

South African Broadcasting Corporation (1996) *This is the SABC*, Johannesburg: Group Communications Directorate of the SABC. Available at: http://www.sabc.co.za [Accessed on: 3 September 2010].

Electronic media — television

After you have studied this chapter, you should be able to:

- ▶ outline the structure of the television newsroom;
- ▶ discuss the functions of the editorial staff and know whom to contact for newsworthy information;
- ▶ assist the television journalist in obtaining information and visual material; and
- ▶ use different programmes for newsworthy information.

Introduction

Audio-visual: using both
sight and sound material

Although television is regarded as the most powerful mass-communication medium because of its *audio-visual* impact, it is also the most difficult medium that the public relations practitioner has to deal with.

Take note

Publicity: public exposure

> *Of the stories submitted to television news by public relations practitioners, 95% are turned down. The main reason for this is that public relations practitioners disregard the newsworthy aspects of the information in favour of promoting a product or institution. Although the main aim of public relations practitioners is to gain publicity for the institution they work for, the focus should still remain on the information's newsworthiness.*

Owing to time constraints and the visual impact of television news, it is often found that bad news has a better chance of being broadcast than good news! Good news is something that normally happens, whereas bad news is abnormal and highlights issues of interest to viewers. Saying this does not mean that public relations practitioners should not endeavour to get 'good news' stories onto television news broadcast. Remember that any item might catch the editor's attention — as long as the information is newsworthy and of public interest.

Television news is not only hard or bad news. It also includes soft news, such as human interest or animal stories Most news bulletins end off with a soft-news story.

This chapter details the newsroom's structure, explaining how the television journalist gathers information and visuals and how this material is prepared for broadcast. We also refer to other programmes that may prove invaluable to public relations practitioners should their information is not appropriate for television news.

Structure of television news

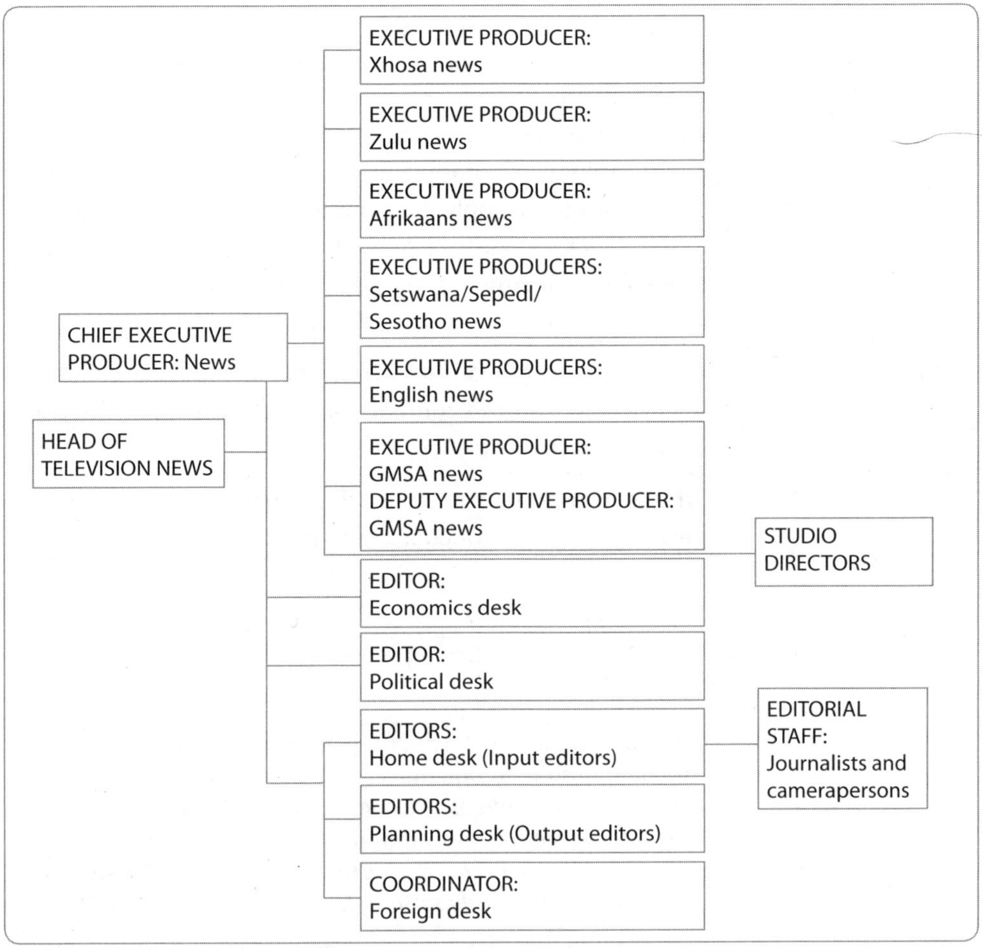

```
CHIEF EXECUTIVE PRODUCER: News ─┬─ EXECUTIVE PRODUCER: Xhosa news
                                ├─ EXECUTIVE PRODUCER: Zulu news
                                ├─ EXECUTIVE PRODUCER: Afrikaans news
                                ├─ EXECUTIVE PRODUCERS: Setswana/Sepedl/Sesotho news
                                ├─ EXECUTIVE PRODUCERS: English news
                                └─ EXECUTIVE PRODUCER: GMSA news / DEPUTY EXECUTIVE PRODUCER: GMSA news ── STUDIO DIRECTORS

HEAD OF TELEVISION NEWS ─┬─ EDITOR: Economics desk
                         ├─ EDITOR: Political desk
                         ├─ EDITORS: Home desk (Input editors) ── EDITORIAL STAFF: Journalists and camerapersons
                         ├─ EDITORS: Planning desk (Output editors)
                         └─ COORDINATOR: Foreign desk
```

Figure 9.1 Television news — editorial structure

Functions of editorial staff

▸ **Head of news** — oversees news gathering and production operations;

▸ **Chief executive producer** — ensures accuracy, fairness, balance of news output as well as coordination between bulletins so that the line-ups of the different language bulletins are similar and also assists the head of news in overseeing news gathering and production operation;

▸ **Home desk** — receives incoming news and decides what news events to cover. Responsible for assigning news stories to journalists;

- **Planning desk** — responsible for planning ahead;
- **Editors** — responsible for overseeing the coverage of events, eg economics, politics;
- **Executive producer** — responsible for content and shape of bulletin;
- **Studio director** — in charge of all studio operations;
- **Journalists** — gather news, uncover stories through interviews and apply their language skills and news sense to get their messages across; and
- **Newsroom staff** — prepare stories filed by journalists for broadcast.

Although each person has his or her own specific duties, the final decision on the contents of bulletins is a joint decision involving each role player.

Why is it important to know the structure of the television newsroom and the functions of its people?

Whom to contact

Let us look at the following scenario:

> *You are employed as a public relations practitioner for a large mining group. An underground rockfall at one of the mines has trapped hundreds of workers and the consequences could be fatal. Since you know that the SABC would be interested in covering this event, you decide to act proactively by contacting the television news department. Whom will you contact?*
>
> *Your contact person is the input editor (indicated in figure 9.1 under 'Editors: Home Desk'). This editor plans the coverage of events for the day. He or she has direct contact with the journalists and will assign one and a camera crew to cover the disaster. If you have already established good relations with a journalist in the television news department, you could inform that person directly and he or she will give the editor all the relevant information. The input editor decides whether the story deserves coverage. If you cannot contact the editor or your contact journalist, you might then contact the chief executive producer of news, who will arrange for a journalist and a camera crew to go out to the mine.*

Public relations practitioners often make the mistake of contacting several news people, eg the chief executive producer, the editor and a journalist, to ensure that the message is received.

Such multiple contacts are not desirable as these people liaise closely with one another. If you reach the editor, he or she will inform all the other role players of the event.

How the television journalist works

Knowledge of how the television journalist covers an event will assist the public relations practitioner in helping the journalist obtain the necessary information and visual material.

Take note

> *The public relations practitioner should see to it that traditional 'Who, What, Where, When, Why and How' questions of journalism (the 5Ws + 1H) can be answered as this will help the journalist to immediately grasp the facts central to the event.*

The public relations practitioner must remember that the journalist is a professional who can judge the news value of a story, distil its essential facts and arrange the information in a way that makes it comprehensible to viewers. This is especially true when the story is fast breaking. Since journalists know what they want, public relations practitioners should be objective and help them obtain all the necessary information, not just what they want to give!

While gathering information, the journalist makes notes. At the same time, the cameraperson will record essential visual material and various other shots that may be used to tell the story. The journalist may also choose people to interview on video.

After the journalist is satisfied with the notes and visual material, he or she may file the report on camera at the scene. This is usually done to close the report.

Back at the office, the journalist and the newsroom staff view and edit the tape. The journalist then writes a script that will be used to mix the direct address made to the camera by the journalist (stand-ups) with the interviews (sound bites).

The newsroom staff then compiles the various packages (reports that need a lead-in by the news anchor) and other items for the bulletin that will be presented by the news anchor (person reading the news). Below is an example of a news bulletin, ie the final product.

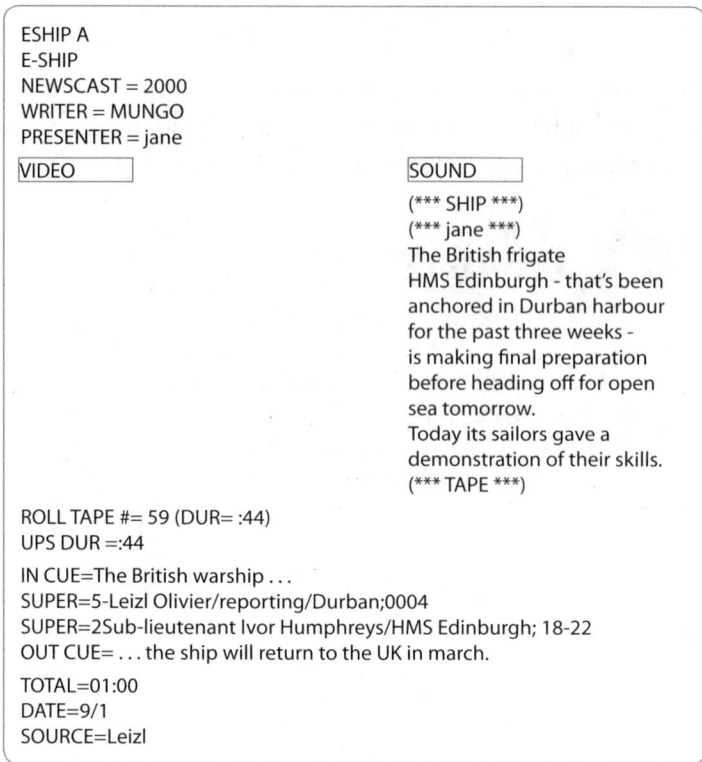

ESHIP A
E-SHIP
NEWSCAST = 2000
WRITER = MUNGO
PRESENTER = jane

VIDEO	SOUND
	(*** SHIP ***)
	(*** jane ***)
	The British frigate
	HMS Edinburgh - that's been
	anchored in Durban harbour
	for the past three weeks -
	is making final preparation
	before heading off for open
	sea tomorrow.
	Today its sailors gave a
	demonstration of their skills.
	(*** TAPE ***)

ROLL TAPE #= 59 (DUR= :44)
UPS DUR =:44

IN CUE=The British warship . . .
SUPER=5-Leizl Olivier/reporting/Durban;0004
SUPER=2Sub-lieutenant Ivor Humphreys/HMS Edinburgh; 18-22
OUT CUE= . . . the ship will return to the UK in march.

TOTAL=01:00
DATE=9/1
SOURCE=Leizl

Figure 9.2 Example of a news bulletin

Now that we have explained how television journalists work, we list some tips for use when dealing with them.

General tips for the public relations practitioner when dealing with television journalists

A television journalist's work is complex. Television news revolves around content and, ultimately, is judged on its picture content. Similarly, the value attributed to news items on any given day is determined by its newsworthiness. For example, if a news conference is scheduled for a certain slot but an unexpected explosion occurs, the news value of the explosion is more than that of the news conference. However, if the news conference was held to announce a new, proactive anti-crime campaign by the national police commissioner, it might still be viewed as the news of the day.

Public relations practitioners are often disappointed when they receive no television coverage for an event that was scheduled. Often the reason is that the initial news value for that day has changed because of other more important events.

Television news falls into the following categories:

- hard news with no visuals;
- hard news with visuals;
- soft news with no visuals; and
- soft news with visuals.

It must be borne in mind that the intrinsic, visual nature of television elevates the importance of visual material. The public relations practitioner must also be able to determine if hard or soft news without visuals will be accepted on the strength of its information alone.

The public relations practitioner's main role is to help the television journalist gather information and visuals. The journalist may need access to forbidden areas, eg a hospital's operating theatre and it is up to the public relations practitioner to arrange access. It should be explained to journalists that they must abide by regulations when entering such areas and if they do not agree, they may be barred from entering.

Television journalists expect transparency from public relations practitioners conveying information. The reportage of journalists has to be *objective*, and the more information — good or bad — that public relations practitioners give, the more trust they generate as a reliable news source.

Objective: facts uncoloured by feelings or opinions

The public relations practitioner, as a spokesperson for an organisation, should have information readily available whether an event is expected or not. He or she should be able to answer any questions since journalists will not provide a list of questions beforehand. Public relations practitioners may ask journalists which angle of the story is being pursued, which gives them a few minutes to prepare such questions.

Although television journalists may spend some time obtaining information and visuals for a news report, only a few minutes are eventually broadcast. This happens even when they cover a scheduled news event taking as long as two to three days. Public relations practitioners should therefore be aware that many hours, even days, may be spent with television journalists for only a few minutes or seconds of broadcast time.

Because of the technical complexity of television news gathering, public relations practitioners must be aware that special provision should sometimes be made to enable television journalists to compile a package. For example, a news conference where an announcement is made about a low-cost housing project may not be visually acceptable to them and they might request to be taken to the area where the houses are to be built. A television crew is therefore handled differently to other media and the situation or event will dictate whether special arrangements need to be made for television. It is not always possible to do so.

However, public relations practitioners should be careful not to give television journalists overly favourable treatment as representatives of the other media might feel that they are favouring television unduly. When giving information, public relations practitioners should ensure that all representatives of the different media receive equal treatment, even if the way in which the information is conveyed differs from one medium to another.

Categories of television programming

In the previous section, one category of television programming, ie news, was discussed. If a public relations practitioner's story is broadcast on a television news bulletin, it can certainly be viewed as a great achievement.

In some cases, you may not be sure whether the information you have is suited to television news. If you are unsure, you should contact the input editor and discuss the matter with him or her. The input editor may see certain aspects of interest that are relevant to the news, or suggest that the information be relayed to another television programme

 **Take note**

Do not make a habit of discussing your stories with input editors. Remember that they have an extremely busy schedule and receive countless telephone calls daily. Do not waste their time and contact only them for advice as a last resort.

Good public relations practitioners should be able to decide whether their stories warrant television coverage. In weighing the options, they should be aware of other programmes that are available.

Television programmes are categorised as follows:

▶ sport;
▶ variety and music;
▶ magazine and documentary;
▶ drama;
▶ religious;
▶ youth and children;
▶ educational; and
▶ ecology.

Deciding on the most appropriate category can be very difficult, and the following criteria must be considered:

▶ **Audience.** This is probably the most important criterion. You need to know who your information is aimed at. Taking the diverse South African markets into consideration, you need to define your audience. If your information is aimed at the youth, you will find a youth programme more appropriate than, for example, a documentary programme.
▶ **Content of message.** The type of information you wish to convey will assist you in deciding the most suitable programme. Your message aimed at the youth may be religious in nature, so another option open to you would be a religious programme. To decide between a youth and a religious programme, the next criterion must be met:
  ▶ **Time.** At what time is the programme broadcast? If you want to target the youth through a religious programme, and these are televised on weekday mornings when scholars are at school, a religious programme is the wrong choice. You must then look at a youth programme televised in the afternoon or early evening.
  ▶ **Language.** This is another very important criterion. If you wish to reach the Zulu-speaking youth and your insert's content is of a religious nature, you will have to find a religious programme or a youth programme presented in that language.

You can see how difficult it is to make the right decision! It is therefore also very important that public relations practitioners use the various sub-departments in the different categories of television programming. They should make contact with the programme organiser to ensure they have made the right decision.

Public relations practitioners must remember that it is possible that, if their information has initial news value, it may be useful for programmes featuring in-depth reportage or debate.

Read the two paragraphs below and discuss the type of programme or programmes you will choose, using the following criteria:

▶ *target group(s);*
▶ *content of message;*
▶ *timeslot; and*
▶ *language.*

1. *As the public relations practitioner of a tertiary educational institution, you wish to inform the potential students about the various educational programmes offered by your institution so that they make the correct career choices. Considering the above criteria, explain how you would choose the correct programme.*

2. *You are the Road Safety Council's public relations practitioner. Because of the many pedestrians killed or injured on the roads, the council has decided to embark on a massive safety awareness campaign. Using the above criteria, what type(s) of television programme(s) do you think would be suitable for this campaign?*

This chapter dealt with the structure of the television newsroom and the editorial staff's functions. Public relations practitioners should know whom to contact at the television newsroom when they have information suited to television news.

Knowledge of how television journalists operate when covering an event is important since public relations practitioners should be aware of their needs.

Although public relations practitioners usually target the newsroom in an effort to gain publicity or to convey information of national interest, they must remember that there may be other programmes suited to promoting their message. When dealing with television journalists and knowing the visual aspects of television journalism, public relations practitioners should be prepared to afford them individual attention.

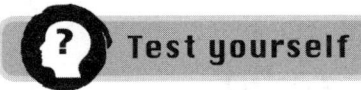 **Test yourself**

1. Outline the structure of the television newsroom and indicate the functions of each editorial staff member.

2. Whom will you contact at the television newsroom when you have newsworthy information?

3. Discuss how television journalists operate when covering an event and explain how the public relations practitioner can assist them.

4. What would your reaction be if a television journalist requests to be treated differently at a news conference? Support your answer by providing reasons.

5. List the various television programmes, other than the news, that the public relations practitioner can use.

6. List and discuss the criteria the public relations practitioner must consider when choosing the most suitable type of programme to use.

Sources consulted

Hyde, SW (1995) *Television & Radio Announcing*, USA: Houghton Mifflin Company.

The television news editorial staff of the SABC.

CHAPTER

10

Electronic media — radio

Objectives

After you have studied this chapter, you should be able to:

▶ discuss the functions of the editorial staff of radio news and know whom to contact with newsworthy information;

▶ assist the radio journalist by providing and gathering information; and

▶ use various radio services and radio programmes to convey newsworthy information.

Introduction

Radio is one of the fastest and most effective mediums to use when the public relations practitioner needs to convey information. One of the most important attributes of radio is that, unlike television, it is portable and is therefore an ideal way to target an audience to gain publicity. Most commuters listen to the radio in the car on their way to and from work. Radio's pitch is therefore different from that of the print media and television in that, although radio messages serve to inform its audiences, its overall aim is to entertain.

The advantages of radio over television and the print media are that radio provides regular news broadcasts on various channels throughout the day. Some radio services broadcast news every hour. Since radio is accessible to most people, especially those in remote areas, its further advantage is that it reaches a largely illiterate audience. Although television also enjoys this advantage, it is not as accessible to such a large audience because it consumes more power and, initially, a television set costs much more than a radio.

As radio is the fastest and most effective means of conveying information to the public, the public relations practitioner must be aware of the time constraints pertaining to messages. If a message needs to reach the public within a specified time, radio is the best medium to use. Although each service has its own timeslots for news broadcasts, regular programmes may be interrupted for special news broadcasts if the information demands it. Take, for example, news of the attempted assassination of a dignitary. This will be broadcast immediately, even if the news is received outside of a scheduled news broadcast as regular programmes can be interrupted to break such news.

Public relations practitioners should acquaint themselves with the news programmes of the various radio services and ascertain these services' target markets. The type of message will to a great extent determine the target audience that needs to hear it.

Although radio news may be more accessible than television news, it is a more difficult medium to use than newspapers. Time is very limited on radio news bulletins and where a few seconds of airtime may be available on television news slots, this may not be the case on radio. Furthermore, because radio listeners are spread over several stations, a message may have to be aired on several stations to reach the desired target audience. Radio listeners cannot go back to go over important points. It is also important to remember that radio is a background medium. Most listeners are doing something else while listening, which means that a message has to work hard to get their attention.

Public relations practitioners must, therefore, be certain of the news value of their information before contacting the radio station. It is also important to distinguish between newsworthy information for national, regional or local radio programmes.

The best way to become acquainted with the radio as a medium is to listen to the various radio services and the programmes they offer. The marketing section or public relations practitioner at the SABC's Radio Services Directorate are good contacts for publications on radio programmes, which are useful as they contain information on the nature of the available radio programmes, what their aims are, and who their target groups are. The Radio Services Directorate also generates statistics detailing and profiling each programme's listenership, which give an indication of the audience that can be reached.

To give the public relations practitioner a basic knowledge of the radio as a mass communication medium, we will discuss the structure of a radio service or station, the newsroom and the editorial staff's functions. We will also look at how radio journalists work and how the public relations practitioner can assist them. Other programmes of use to the public relations practitioner, such as talk shows and actuality programmes, are also mentioned.

Structure of the radio service

Studying the structure of public service radio, will show how a radio service's various departments can be of use to public relations. In the following diagram the departments and the programmes available in each department are illustrated.

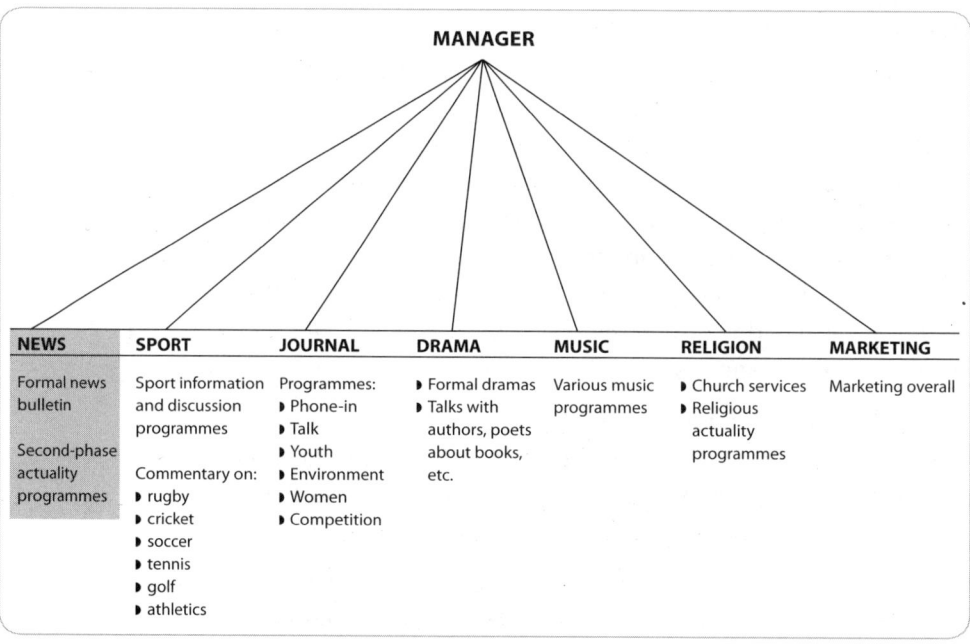

Figure 10.1 Public service radio

Take note

Each of the departments shown in the diagram on page 114 is run by a producer and each programme within the department has an announcer. Announcers constantly look for stories and information to use in their programmes and public relations practitioners must decide where their information fits in.

In the following section, we focus on the news department, where formal news bulletins and second-phase actuality programmes feature. (See the grey area in figure 10.1.) We will then discuss how other programmes can be used by the public relations practitioner.

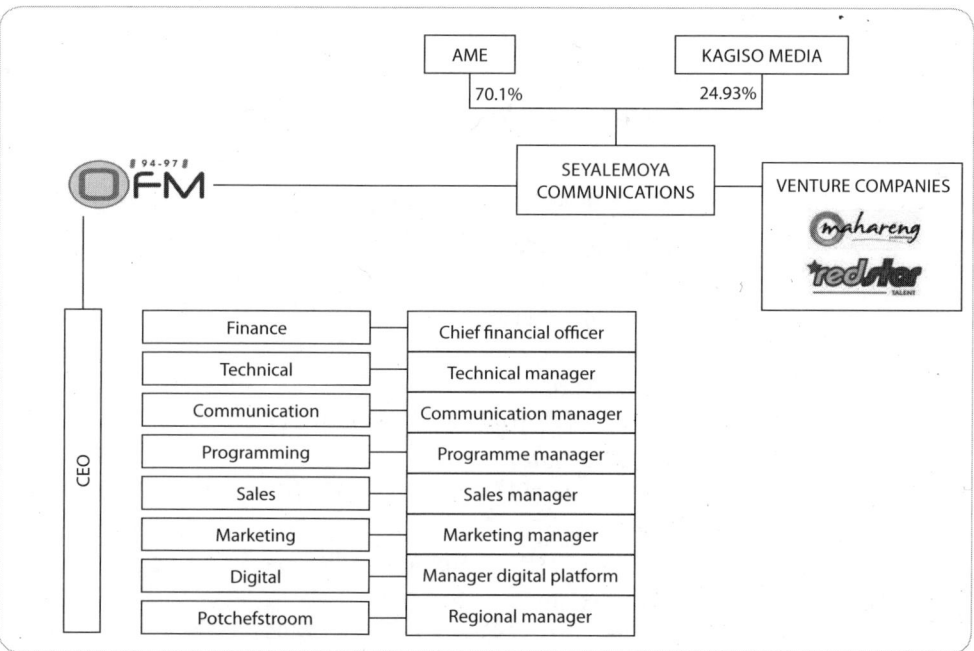

Figure 10.2 Organogram 2010-03-25 (courtesy of OFM)

Radio newsroom

Radio news and actuality programmes are compiled by editorial staff including executive producers, editors, senior journalists, journalists and junior journalists.

The functions of the editorial staff

- **Executive producers** control the news and actuality programmes and are responsible for all the news bulletins and actuality programmes broadcast on the various services.
- **Editors** are responsible for specific programmes and decide what will be broadcast. Editors are also responsible for quality control.
- **Senior journalists** are responsible for in-depth reports.
- **Journalists and junior journalists** are responsible for the daily gathering of newsworthy information and may also do investigative journalism.

Radio news regional editors

Regional radio is an important outlet for radio news. There are nine local regions to which news from those areas can be broadcast. In these regions, regional editors decide what information is to be used in news bulletins.

> **The regional radio news offices**
>
> **Gauteng – Johannesburg**
> Tel: (011) 714 9111; Fax: (011) 714 9744
>
> **Gauteng – Pretoria**
> Tel: (012) 431 5300; Fax: (012) 431 5490
>
> **Western Cape**
> Tel: (021) 430 8100; Fax: (021) 430 8411
>
> **KwaZulu-Natal**
> Tel: (031) 362 5111; Fax: (031) 362 5100
>
> **Free State**
> Tel: (051) 503 3111; Fax: (051) 503 3264
>
> **Eastern Cape**
> Tel: (041) 391 1255; Fax: (041) 373 1406
>
> **Limpopo**
> Tel: (015) 290 0269; Fax: (015) 290 0178/9
>
> **Mpumalanga**
> Tel: (013) 759 6600; Fax: (013) 755 2823
>
> **Northern Cape**
> Tel: (053) 802 5800; Fax: (053) 802 5948
>
> **North West**
> Tel: (018) 389 7111; Fax: (018) 389 7299

Whom to contact·

If public relations practitioners have well-established contacts in the newsroom, they may contact the relevant journalist directly, who will in turn brief the editor. Alternatively, public relations practitioners may contact the news editor, who will have a journalist contact them for the information. The same rules applicable to television apply here — do not contact various people in an effort to have information broadcast.

If public relations practitioners have information of regional value, the person to contact is the regional editor.

How the radio journalist works

The radio journalist has the same responsibilities as the print journalist in terms of collecting, collating and then reporting the news in a local, national or worldwide capacity. A good radio journalist will typically use interviews, press conferences and sound effects to make listeners feel as though they are also on the scene. The difference between radio journalism and other forms of journalism is that a radio report is often heard once and then it is gone, so radio journalists have to make sure that their stories are concise, brief and easily understood. Like a television journalist, a radio journalist often presents the news live (*Wisegeek.com*).

Public relations practitioners should know how radio journalists work and what their requirements are when covering an event or when gathering information.

It is as important for the radio journalist as for journalists from any other medium to gather information according to the traditional 5Ws + 1H (Who, What, When, Where, Why and How). Since airtime is limited, answers to these questions can help the radio journalist summarise events quickly and compile a radio report based on the salient facts.

Radio journalists often use a portable cassette recorder when gathering information. When someone is being interviewed on television, many microphones are usually visible in front of the person, most of which belong to radio journalists who are recording the interview. Radio journalists also write information in a notebook and use the telephone to get information.

They write the report in a standard format and style and hand it to the news editor. As radio news is written for the ear, short sentences and simple language are used.

A news bulletin is compiled from the various stories received from journalists and is then read by the studio's anchor person. The following is an extract from such a news bulletin. It represents the result of the interaction between the public relations practitioner and the journalist.

IN THIS NEWS BULLETIN.........

The police keep a close watch on the Free State Technikon campus AND .... The students of the University of Zululand protest against increased tuition fees. DETAILS COMING UP

---

bfntech

The Free State Technikon campus is tense this morning with a strong police presence on the campus. A police spokesperson says that they will arrest anyone who contravenes an interdict prohibiting the disruption of lectures on campus. Earlier today about 200 students waited outside the administrative buildings. However, there have been no reports of incidents.

---

boycott

Students of the University of Zululand are staging a one day boycott in protest against increased tuition fees. They're also unhappy about the failure of tertiary institutions in KwaZulu-Natal to admit all students. Students are picketing and chanting songs on the university campus.

anthony, nelspruit/korrie mthethwa 21/02 pks/ metro

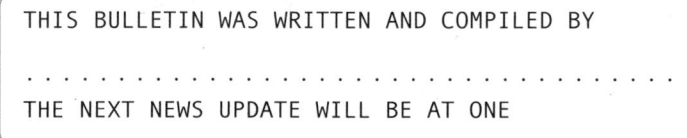

```
THIS BULLETIN WAS WRITTEN AND COMPILED BY

. . . . . . . . . . . . . . . . . . . . . . . . . . . . . . . . . . . . . . . .

THE NEXT NEWS UPDATE WILL BE AT ONE
```

Figure 10.3 Extract from a news bulletin

When a journalist uses a tape recorder, eg while interviewing a doctor about a new surgical procedure, the information can be used in two ways. The journalist can listen to the taped interview and write a story using the most important points. Alternatively, the taped interview can be edited in the studio before being presented as part of a current affairs or actuality programme. Radio news bulletins do not usually include recorded interviews although one or two sentences might be included in the bulletin, but only if the interview gives a news story additional impact.

Take note

Another way to gather and convey information is by reporting 'live'. Radio journalists are usually equipped with a cellphone when on a live reporting assignment. The journalist is then linked to the news anchor in the studio by telephone and the report is broadcast live. This type of reporting is appropriate for actuality or current affairs programmes, but can be used effectively in normal news slots if the event warrants it. For example, a huge mountain blaze endangering people's lives can be described by a reporter against the backdrop of wailing fire-truck sirens, creating a 'word picture' in the listeners' mind. Such reportage of dangerous situations has immense impact on a news slot.

Categories of radio programming

Although public relations' efforts are directed mainly at news bulletins, there are other programmes that public relations practitioners can use just as effectively. Figure 10.1 illustrates departments focusing on sport, journal, drama, music and religion, which public relations practitioners can use in order to decide if their information is of use to any of the programmes in these departments. It is therefore important to understand the format of radio stations. Following is an overview of the types of format on SABC radio stations (*AfriMAP 2010*):

Types of format

Radio stations have news, current affairs and informational programmes, some of which include phone-in programmes. Music and talk-show formats tend to dominate the public commercial stations. Radio 2000 has struggled to identify its niche, but was repositioned in April 2008 to include a mix of music and public service content and to prepare it for its role as the official SABC radio broadcaster for the 2010 FIFA World Cup. The main format for the public service programmes are interviews combined with phone-in programmes.

The public commercial stations mostly opt for a contemporary hit radio format. 5 FM relies mainly on music programmes fronted by prominent disk jockeys and may also include interviews and a live phone-in component, as well as humorous, controversial skits. Metro FM offers a mix of music and radio talk-show formats, as well as a dedicated radio talk show on sport. Goodhope FM is described by the SABC as an interactive lifestyle radio station, which includes a mix of R&B, pop, ballads, contemporary jazz and dance and old school music.

The SABC public service radio stations offer a mix of formats. Given that most of the African-language radio stations claim to target the 16–49 age group in the main, they opt mostly (but not exclusively) for talk-show and music formats. Ukhozi FM and Umhlobo Wenene offer news and current affairs, interactive phone-in talk shows, sport, weather and traffic. Music covers a spread of genres, including jazz, R&B, kwaito, house, gospel and traditional African music.

- Lesedi FM offers news, information, talk and drama, music appealing to the youth, as well as gospel and seSotho traditional and contemporary music.
- As Ligwalagwala FM seeks to target a younger, more upwardly mobile audience, its line-up offers news and current affairs, education (including phone-in learner support programmes), music and talk-show formats.

- Motsweding claims to be a highly interactive station offering news, current affairs, music, phone-in programmes, education, sport, weather and traffic.
- Mughana Lonene and Phalaphala rely heavily on music and talk-show formats (with the former offering 80% local music), while Thobela FM offers music, information, education and entertainment. Faith-based programmes involving interviews with prominent religious leaders are also included in many of the stations' line-ups, as are public service announcements.
- As Tru FM aims to target a young upwardly mobile consumerist audience, it relies heavily on music and talk-show formats.

English-language SAfm relies heavily on talk radio shows hosted by popular anchors, with live interactive programming dominating the schedule. Afrikaans-language Radio Sonder Grense uses similar formats, but plays more music than SAfm does. Current affairs programmes of one to two hours duration, including live interviews with key newsmakers, are flighted in the morning, at lunchtime and in the afternoon. Lotus FM, which targets the Indian community, uses a music and talk-show format.

Channel Africa broadcasts on shortwave and the Internet and calls itself 'The Voice of the African Renaissance'.

The following illustrates how different programmes can be used:

You are the public relations practitioner in the Ministry of Environmental Affairs, Water Affairs and Forestry. The minister is about to announce the building of a new dam.

The Minister's initial announcement is hard news and therefore important material for a news bulletin. First, contact the news editor, who will assign a journalist to the story. The news broadcast can then be followed by an actuality programme where, for example, people speculate on how the dam will affect their living standards.

You can go further and contact the environmental programme announcer. Offer the announcer a talk with authorities on the merits of building the dam. Now you can telephone the announcer of the talk-radio journal programme. Arrangements can be made to invite an expert to tell listeners how the dam will be built, etc.

This example illustrates how a single announcement, ie the building of a dam, can be used in several programmes. The minister's initial announcement was hard news. This was followed by second-phase journalism in the actuality programme and the softer story describing how the dam would be built. The secret is to think laterally — a single story has many sides.

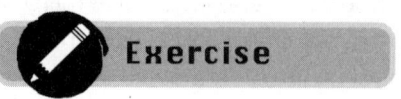

Following the adoption of a new Constitution on 8 May 1996, you must arrange radio interviews and radio talk-shows for members of the Constitutional Assembly (CA) to inform the nation of the historic significance the constitution holds for the country. Furthermore, several constitutional experts who assisted the CA draft the new Constitution are available for radio talk shows.

Using the diagram of public service radio, list the programme types that you will use for the case study above:

Time schedules

Public relations practitioners should note that radio works according to the clock, as does television. If a programme is scheduled for 08:00, then it starts at 08:00. If you have arranged for a spokesperson to be at the studio at 08:10, see to it that the person arrives at the studio at 07:50. Not only will the person be in time for the interview, he or she will also have time to relax.

Punctuality and readiness also apply when you or a spokesperson is scheduled to record a telephone interview. The journalist or announcer will arrange to telephone you at a set time to record the interview — make sure that you are waiting for the call.

How public relations practitioners can assist radio journalists

It is important to realise that journalists from the electronic and print media all have their own requirements.

Television is technologically complex, requiring sound and vision. Radio journalists work with sound only. If the radio journalist wants to interview the public relations practitioner or the head of the organisation, the public relations practitioner must allow for the fact that the journalist will need a quiet area to record the interview and arrange a quiet venue for it.

When journalists telephone you for information and do not use a tape recorder, give them the necessary information so that they can write a report for use in a news bulletin.

If a radio journalist telephones you to request a telephonic interview to be recorded in the studio, ensure that no interruptions take place during the interview. Root (2009) offers the following techniques for successful radio interviews:

Prepare but do not over-prepare

▶ You will want to sound knowledgeable, intelligent and even likable. Anticipate as many of the questions as you can and prepare answers for the more difficult ones. It is important to practise how you want to present your information, both in terms of the content and the tone. Practise a smooth delivery and avoid sounding as if you are caught off-guard by questions.

▶ You do not, however, want to sound like a well-rehearsed radio commercial. You want the conversation to seem spontaneous because this can add to the notion that you have a good understanding of your business and how it operates. Take a moment to formulate your answer properly so the response sounds intelligent and try to make the conversation sound natural and unrehearsed.

Phone-in shows

▶ Sometimes a radio station will want to allow the audience to get involved in the interview by opening up the show to phone calls. The radio station will arrange this with you in advance and if you are given the chance to speak to the public, take it. A phone-in show will allow you to put any popular misconceptions about your company to rest and will allow potential customers to hear how helpful you can be. Take notes on who called in and what they asked. Note how you answered a question and if a customer has requested a follow-up, make sure you do so.

Ensure that more time is spent with callers on their question than on your answer. Make your answer brief and to the point and avoid allowing callers a rebuttal to your response. Avoid confrontations. If a call seems to be heading this way, end it as quickly and professionally as you can.

Have your message ready

▶ You may not get many chances to get your message out on the radio, so have a few statements prepared that will help you sum up your business. Interviewers' questions may not cover everything you want, so prepare them so they can ask the proper questions. Keep your statement short but informative. If the interviewer has hit upon the topics you would like to cover, expand on your company's offerings and use the interview to your advantage.

Securing radio interviews

Securing radio interviews is a common challenge faced by many public relations practitioners. Consider the following when attempting to get radio publicity interviews as an interview guest to promote your organisation:

▶ Identify radio shows that book guests for interviews.
▶ Find contact information for the radio show's producers.
▶ Create and send a targeted pitch — call the producers to offer information that is new. Your pitch should be aimed at getting their attention and should fit into their current radio show programming needs.

Placing your message or corporate advertisement on radio

Planning is crucial should public relations practitioners consider placing messages or corporate advertisements on radio. They should be fully informed about how radio functions and be familiar with the key personnel associated with radio. Consider the following (adapted from *Entrepreneur.com*) when planning to place your message or corporate advertisement on air (remember that newsworthy messages are free publicity while corporate advertisements are paid for):

▶ **Establish your target market** by asking yourself who your customers are and therefore whom you want to reach. This may seem obvious, but ensure that you pitch your message or corporate advertisement on the correct station and programme so that you always reach the intended target audience.

▶ **Set a rough budget that is reasonable.** Many stations suggest running corporate advertisements for at least three months, but this may be costly. Radio does, however, cost less although rates vary widely depending on the size of the market, the station's penetration and the audience of the show on which you want to advertise.

▶ **Contact sales managers at television and radio stations in your area.** This is to gather information and become familiar with list of available spots on shows during hours that you want to reach your target audience.

▶ **Ask about the 'audience delivery' of the available spots and calculate the cost per thousand (CPM) of reaching your target audience.** Remember, you are buying an audience, not just time on a show, and you can calculate an approximate amount of how much it is going to cost you to reach your target audience.

▶ **Compare the various proposals.** Look at the CPMs and negotiate the most attractive deal based on which outlet offers the most cost-effective way of reaching your audience. Buying time well in advance can help lower the cost.

 **Take note**

When you send a news release to radio news, do not include a photograph. It will not be used. It might sound ridiculous, but some public relations practitioners do send visual material to radio stations, to the great amusement of radio personnel! As a public relations practitioner, you should act professionally at all times — never give the media reason to develop a low opinion of your profession.

Summary

Knowledge of the newsroom's structure and the editorial staff's functions will assist the public relations practitioner in conveying information to radio news.

Public relations practitioners should always be aware that radio provides various publicity opportunities. News bulletins fall into only one category that can be used. Public relations practitioners should acquaint themselves with the many radio services and radio programmes that can be used most effectively.

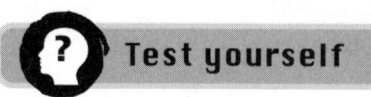

Test yourself

You are the public relations practitioner at a hospital where conjoined twins were successfully separated. Since this type of operation usually poses great risks, the fact that both patients survived the operation is already of great significance. Keeping in mind that this is newsworthy (and could generate interest in other programmes), discuss how you will go about informing radio services' news departments and other programmes of your choice. You must indicate specific radio services you will use for the news angle and those that you will use for the human-interest angle. Support your choices by providing reasons.

Sources consulted

AfriMAP's 2010 overview of the SABC (2010) Available at: http://www.communitymedia. org.za/alt-media-resources/128?start=3 [Accessed on:]

Entrepreneur.com, Available at: http://www.entrepreneur.com/advertising/adsbytype/ broadcastads/article21746 [Accessed on: 19 September 2010]

Radio and TV advertising — Turn up the volume on your ad campaign by adding radio and television spots to the mix. (2004) Available at: http://www.entrepreneur.com/advertising/ adsbytype/broadcastads/article21746 [Accessed on: 19 September 2010]

Root, GN (2009) *Radio interview techniques.* Available at: http://www.ehow.com/ way_5201801_radio-interview-techniques.html [Accessed on: 31 August 2010]

Staff members from radio stations, SABC.

Wisegeek.com. Available at: http://www.wisegeek.com/how-do-i-become-a-journalist. htm [Accessed on: 7 August 2010]

What does a radio journalist do? Available at: http://www.wisegeek.com/what-does-a-radio-journalist-do.htm [Accessed on: 5 September 2010]

'New media'

Objectives

After you have studied this chapter, you should be able to:

▶ define the concept 'new media';

▶ explain what the advent of Internet, e-mail, the World Wide Web, mailing lists and news groups represent in communications; and

▶ discuss in detail how public relations practitioners apply new media in executing their technical role.

Introduction

In this millennium, public relations practitioners, along with other communications practitioners such as journalists, will not be able to do their jobs professionally and resourcefully without using new media tools. This chapter provides a brief introduction to the concept of 'new media' and what it entails. Technology and its various applications change almost daily. It is up to you to keep abreast of these changes and to adapt your work situation and needs accordingly. The aim of this chapter is to create an awareness of the existence of new media tools and to encourage you to make use of them, especially in your dealings with the mass communication media. Using these tools will enhance your knowledge of new technology and will provide you with time-saving communication with the representatives of the various mass-communication media.

However much the application of new media tools may provide you with faster and more efficient communication, it is important not to neglect face-to-face contact, especially when dealing with journalists.

What is 'new media'?

The term 'new media' was coined to differentiate between the *old* media world of print, radio and television and the *new* media world of computerised electronic publishing using a multimedia combination of print, audio, video and digital images on the Internet and other digital formats such as CD-ROM and DVD.

CD-ROM: a compact disk (CD) with read-only memory

The arrival of this new technology in the1990s radically transformed every aspect of communication, including how we communicate, where we communicate and with whom we communicate.

DVD versatile disk or digital video disk: a new type of CD-ROM that holds a minimum of 4.7 gigabytes (GB), enough for a full-length movie

The most obvious place to start when discussing new media is the Internet and the World Wide Web. E-mail, mailing lists and news groups are, however, other members of the new media that are emerging as regular public relations tools. Furthermore, the wireless and mobile communications revolution has taken the communications industry out of the office and into the real world.

Digital mobile equipment, including cellphones, iPods and palm-top computers, form an integral part of this growing innovation. Wireless technology has fast become an indispensable tool in the weaponry of public relations practitioners, journalists and other communications practitioners.

McLuhan's global village

It seems that the world has moved amazingly close to realising Marshall McLuhan's global village. In his book, *The Medium is the Message*, which was first published in 1967, McLuhan states that we live in a global village where things happen simultaneously all over the world. Time and space no longer have any significance.

McLuhan maintains that the electronic media involves people all over the world simultaneously. He says the electronic media puts us back in touch with the ancestral emotions from which print (books, newspapers and magazines) has divorced us.

Not only is there a new multisensory view of the world, but people from countries around the world can communicate as if they all live in the same village.

When McLuhan outlined this global village vision more than 40 years ago, the Internet, the World Wide Web, cellphones and other modern-day digital gadgets did not exist. However, the World Wide Web, more than any other medium, brings his prediction to fulfilment.

The Web provides the means for diverse people to communicate their messages to the rest of the world. Every site on the World Wide Web is available to anyone who has a computer and a modem.

Time and space become insignificant, as a click can take you to a site halfway around the world. Through search engines such as *Yahoo* and *Google*, it presents a web of interconnected documents straddling the globe. Thus, the Web becomes the global village square, where everyone meets to communicate and exchange information.

The 20th century saw the invention of telephone, radio and wireless communication, television, the computer, satellite communication, the Internet and the World Wide Web, cellphones, etc. Each of these inventions has played a major role in revolutionising communications

Public relations and the new media

Let us investigate how public relations practitioners can use new media technology to improve the service they provide as company journalists or as public relations consultants.

When we compare old and new media in public relations, we find things have changed dramatically.

While the *computer* is still the core tool used in the process of gathering and passing on information in a public relations landscape, tools such as *digital cameras, optical scanners* and *cellphones* are enabling practitioners to publicise their company faster and more efficiently and over a wider spectrum.

The methods used to collect information, the way we interpret the information we gather and the mode of transmission of electronic information have all changed significantly.

Digital camera: a camera that stores images digitally rather than recording them on film. Once a picture has been taken with the camera, it can be downloaded to a computer system

Optical scanner: a device that can read text and illustrations that are printed on paper, and translate the information into a form the computer can use

Single-level presentations, ie using a speaker to address the media during a public relations product presentation and afterwards giving the media representatives a press kit, formed part of the 'old' media world. Nowadays, with the sophisticated technology available to communication practitioners, information is presented in a multilayered fashion to a target audience using a combination of video, audio, text and data. Furthermore, the audience can watch the presentation and even participate in the event from another continent thousands of kilometres away, due to the interactive quality of the new media.

You can literally reach a global audience instantly. Your target audience can log on to the Internet, search the World Wide Web, participate in an interactive multimedia tour of your facility or watch a pre-recorded video of your specific service or product. They can read about the latest international research done on your product, view digital photographs of it and listen via 'streaming' audio to a number of experts in the field discussing the findings of the new research. Visitors to your company website can even post their own electronic messages to the experts via e-mail and receive immediate responses.

The advantages and disadvantages of new media

Advantages

- The new media technologies make it increasingly easy to access vast amounts of information, not only in the office but also while on the move. With the new wireless equipment on the market, it is even possible for the public relations office to be mobile.
- Owing to its mobility, new media technology facilitates communication between people from all walks of life.
- Information can be gathered and then distributed to the media much faster.
- Picture material is available on demand.
- Target marketing and audience specialisation is possible.
- It is ultimately cheaper.
- It is more user friendly and interactive.

Disadvantages

- Potential health risks associated with electromagnetic radiation.
- The possible erosion of the world's literacy rate.
- Piracy of electronic information.
- Growing social fragmentation.
- Division between the information rich and the information poor.
- The formation of an information underclass.

What exactly is the Internet?

The Internet, once an almost surrealistic concept, has now become a business tool that could be one of the most useful communication devices used by the public relations practitioner.

The US Defence Force devised the Internet, which is often referred to as 'the global information superhighway', about three decades ago to act as a communication system for the exchange of scientific data and intelligence.

After the National Science Foundation Network joined the system and linked the Internet to universities and research bodies, it just grew and grew and today it is accessible to everyone.

Because of its defence force beginnings, many people think that it is still controlled by the military, but this is not true at all. No one is actually in charge of the Internet. There are huge firms who have put certain structures in place to facilitate the whole process but no one particular body, company or country is in charge of the Internet.

Anyone can put anything on the Internet and, although 99% of surfers (people who use the Internet) are decent people, there is a small element that uses it for less savoury activities such as pornography and selling illegal items.

Internet users must be aware that they must obey the laws of the country in which they reside.

The Internet is a wonderfully easy way to distribute information about a company, to issue news releases (with pictures, if desired) and to gather information.

What is needed to use the Internet?

- A computer, and
- A telephone connection or wire-less 3G connection.
- A modem, which is the device that allows one computer talk to another via a telephone line. Modems come as a card that fits within a computer or as an external box, which plugs into a computer port. Incidentally, a modem will also enable faxes to be sent and received straight from a computer.
- An Internet service provider, which is an organisation that sells access to the Internet. For a monthly fee, they will provide a connection with their server. This includes access to e-mail and possibly space for a personal web page. Some organisations provide Internet access free to their clients. For instance, Absa bank in South Africa provided free Internet access to their clients early in 2001.

What is on the Internet?

The Internet is vast. You can find almost everything you could ever wish to know or want on it. If what you are looking for exists, then the chances are that it will be stored somewhere on the Internet.

Because the cost is quite reasonable (the charge is the fee of a local (national) telephone call, even if you are searching a data-base in, for example, the US or Europe), you are able to do a really thorough search on any topic. However, information is not the only thing of use on the Internet.

You can order or download almost anything you need through the Internet. You can, for example, download free software or order new hardware, and buy books, music, clothes, shoes, cars, houses or any other item. There are up-to-date news bulletins and weather charts, interviews to listen to, pictures to view or download, information on celebrities, etc. All you have to do is find it.

The Internet is just a physical connection. It is utilised as a global communication system using the following key tools:

- the World Wide Web;
- e-mail;
- listservs or mailing lists;
- newsgroups; and
- chat.

The World Wide Web

The World Wide Web (WWW) forms part of the Internet, giving it a face and making it easier to access the unimaginably huge amounts of information stored on it. The WWW can almost be described as an index of sorts.

For example, when looking up information on a certain topic, you might have 3 000 references about it. Instead of downloading each article in its entirety, the search will give the first paragraph or so and refer you to a web address.

Many companies have their own web pages and addresses, and public relations practitioners would do well to ensure that their company is also represented in this way. These web pages can easily be made up so that the rest of the world can access them.

What is needed to use the World Wide Web?

You need full Internet access through an Internet provider service or a direct line into your network to be able to use WWW. You also need software to browse the web. This software translates the hypertext mark-up language (html) used to create web pages and displays it on your computer screen in a readable and usable way. Many different browsers have been developed, but the two main ones used in most countries in the world, including South Africa, are Netscape and Microsoft's Internet Explorer. Both have similar functions.

Searching the World Wide Web

One of the main reasons people use the Internet is to access information. Owing to the decentralised nature of the WWW and the enormous amount of information available, it can be very difficult to find the exact information that you are looking for as it is updated every day. In January 2000, the WWW surpassed a billion web pages. Because of the vast number of web pages, finding specific information can be like finding the proverbial needle in a haystack. In order to locate information on the web, *search tools* are used. These perform searches of the Internet based on the input of the user and could include keywords, topics and phrases. Search tools are becoming more powerful and sophisticated every year. Because of the enormous amount of information out there, they are indispensable.

Search tools

Search tools are divided into two main categories, namely search engines and categorised Internet Search Directories.

Search engines

Examples of well-known search engines are:

- Google;
- Yahoo;
- Ask;
- Lycos; and
- AOL Search.

South African search engines

Popular South African search engines include *Ananzi, Aardvark, Max* and *MWEB*.

Exercise

Nielsen monitors and measures more than 90% of global Internet activity and provides insights about the online universe — including audiences, advertising, video, e-commerce and consumer behaviour. Log on to the Nielsen homepage (http://www.nielson.com) and list the latest global search engine ratings.

There are probably thousands of search engines and directories on the WWW, most of them free to the user. They are able to provide a free service because they make their money through selling advertising or offering additional premium services. There are different types of search engines, including human-generated indexes, spider-generated indexes, non-web protocol search sites, meta-search engines and web rings.

Most search engines and search directories provide the following tools to help you find what you are looking for:

- a search form to enter your query;
- ways to broaden or narrow the extent of your search; and
- a results list of pages that match your query.

The search engine usually produces a ranked list where the documents at the top of the list have more relevance than those toward the bottom. This is based on how many of the search terms are present in the document, how frequently the search terms occur and how close the search terms are to one another.

E-mail

E-mail is the tool that you, as a public relations practitioner, would use most frequently to get your company's news to the media. More than 15 million people in more than 40 countries send and receive electronic messages around the world on the Internet.

Until recently, public relations practitioners used either faxes or hard copies of a news release to inform the media about newsworthy events or developments. However, e-mail is both faster and cheaper than fax and phone and will eventually step into the shoes of fax. E-mail is fast becoming the chosen method of communication for businesses that will rely on it as a form of communication as they now rely on telephonic communication.

Every Internet user has an e-mail address, which ensures that your e-mail does not float around in cyberspace but reaches you safe and sound through your computer. It also ensures privacy, as a password is usually needed to retrieve it. Since the advent of e-mail, the ordinary, hand-delivered post is often now referred to as 'snail mail' (as it is so much slower).

The advantages of e-mail is that the people you want to contact are able to receive their mail seconds or minutes after it has been sent and not days later. In addition, you, as a public relations practitioner, can send the same news release and pictures to a host of different addresses at the same time. You can even ask for confirmation that the mail has been received by the parties to whom it was sent.

The e-mail system can be used internally, ie within an organisation, to distribute important notices, memos, newsletters, etc. Using e-mail in this way often alleviates the need to have frequent physical meetings in order to have memos, news releases and other articles cleared by superiors before they are released.

In companies with several branches scattered throughout the country, e-mail is a cost-effective communication tool.

Internet mailing lists

Internet mailing lists allow people with similar interests to communicate easily with each other via e-mail. People subscribe to a mailing list, usually free of charge and can then send a single message to the list that is automatically

E-mail: the abbreviated form of electronic mail, which is the transmission of messages over a communication network. Such messages can be notes entered straight from the computer keyboard or electronic files stored on a disk distributed to all other list subscribers. These mailing lists are often referred to as listservs. Popular mailing lists include *Listproc* and *Majordomo*.

Mailing lists are used by media practitioners to find expert sources and locate 'regular people' who can help them find particular information. There are many public relations- and journalism-related lists that are used to help keep abreast of different facets of the profession.

Search the WWW and find a few mailing lists that interest you. Search the Web for the Institute of Public Relations and join their mailing list. As a future public relations practitioner, joining this list holds many benefits. Log on to http://www.instituteforpr.org

Newsgroups

Newsgroups are electronic bulletin boards on the Internet. An estimated 300 000 messages are posted on more than 60 000 newsgroups on the WWW daily. Newsgroups can help communications practitioners find specific people, identify expert sources and listen to conversations of interest groups.

Deja is a popular newsgroup that allows users to search more than three years' worth of archives. Searches can be conducted by topic, author or e-mail address.

Search the WWW and find at least 30 newsgroups that would interest you. Try to contact one. List the names of the newsgroups you chose.

Chat and instant messaging

The option of making use of chat rooms for more informal communication creates the possibility to communicate worldwide with very little effort. Chat rooms enable you to link directly with anyone who is at the same chat room at the same time as yourself.

Instant messaging software and programmes allow you to 'talk' to people in real time by typing and receiving messages. Instant messaging, or IM, is becoming increasingly popular for both personal and business use. These days, most IM programmes can be accessed via the computer and cellphone. Advanced IM software programmes also allow the use of rich media such as live voice and video calling, facilitated by the use of webcams.

Examples include the following:

▶ MXit — a popular South African chat software, most widely accessible via cellphones;
▶ *Twitter*, *Facebook* and *MySpace* — social network sites, that have built-in IM chat software; and
▶ *Google*, *Yahoo* and *MSN* — search engines that all have their own IM software programmes that enable real time conversations, with the enhanced options of voice and video calling.

Online media

Where to start?

> *She is woken by the alarm on her PDA and checks her e-mail and a couple of podcasts while having a cup of coffee. Then she races off to her office, which is actually the spare bedroom in her apartment. After adjusting the webcam and microphone on her desktop, she chimes into her first meeting of the day with fellow account executives in Africa as well as some of her colleagues in the US. An instant message from a reporter pops up on her screen while she watches a real-time PowerPoint presentation on the best way to launch her client's new social networking site (adapted from Kelleher 2007:2).*

PDA: a personal digital assistant or palmtop computer is a mobile device that includes a telephone, a media player and Internet access functions

Podcast: also known as a non-streamed webcast is a series of digital media files released for download through web-syndication

The vignette on page 137 describes how changes in media technology continue to affect the practice of public relations. The online media landscape is ever-changing, with new technology being developed at an increasingly fast rate. In order to stay connected with their public, public relations practitioners need to keep abreast of changing technologies.

In the public relations profession, online communication is essential. Online public relations is more a matter of what people are doing with online media technologies than what these technologies are doing to people.

Websites, e-mail, intranets, Internet forums, wikis and blogs look and act completely differently to the media of early mass-communication research such as newspapers, books, radio and television. Online media cover a broad range of communication systems, channels and formats. The Internet is *the* medium for online communication. All the elements of Internet communication technology are termed *online media* (Kelleher 2007).

Following is an set of definitions adapted from Kelleher (2007):

- **Uniform resource locators (URLs)** are the working Internet addresses for Web resources, which can include audio files, video text and pictures.
- **File transfer protocol (FTP)** allows users to put files on a computer server that other people can retrieve from different locations.
- **Intranets** are networked information systems that an organisation hosts for its internal publics. Users require a password and must be registered to participate, for example, an organisation's staff portal that requires a registered username and password to gain access.
- **Content management systems (CMS)** are computer software systems for organising and facilitating the joint creation of documents and other content. For example, *Wikipedia* is a CMS, and people around the world can register and edit its content.
- **Wikis** are a type of website that allows users to easily add, remove or edit all content quickly and easily, sometimes without the need for registration.

- **Blogs** are websites that contain online personal journals with reflections, comments and often hyperlinks provided by the writers. A blog is a form of interpersonal communication, for example *e-blogger, Xanga, LiveJournal, WordPress* and *Vox*.
- **Feeds** and really simple syndication (RSS) carry messages such as text-based blog entries or audiovisual files that are syndicated to subscribers online after they are posted. Feeds downloaded to iPods and other digital media players are called *podcasts*.
- **Social networks** focus on building online communities of people who share interests and/or activities or who want to explore the interests and activities of others. Most social network services are web based and provide a variety of ways for users to interact, such as e-mail and instant messaging services. Apart from the Internet connection fee, these websites do not charge a hosting fee. Public relations practitioners can thus be creative in how they use such websites to generate free publicity. Examples are *Facebook, MySpace* and *Twitter*.

The impact of new media technology on the public relations profession

These days, computers, cellphones and BlackBerries are not only used for work, but also as integral ways of managing lives. 'New and social media' has become one of the main reasons that people access the Internet. People want a way to engage with one another and websites that allow interaction. CNN recently reported on the release of Apple's iPad and that the sales reached 300 units on the first day. Other CNN programmes regularly feature stories on the use of new and social media. For example, an Asian women's plight was carried on via new media even though she was held under house arrest without access to any phones or computers. On another programme, the possibility of using social media to interact and contribute to a country's demographic governance was discussed.

Thus, contrary to the media's characterisation, *Twitter* and *Facebook* are not just places to read celebrities' blogs and meet new people. Students of all ages need to understand more about this fascinating communication channel.

New media technologies allow for the multidirectional flow of information, targeting many people across different parts of the world. Earlier communication models placed emphasis on the *sender* of the information, but newer communication models stress the importance of the *receiver*. This shift in power means that public relations practitioners need to keep abreast of changing media technologies in order to *stay* connected with existing target publics and *attract* new target publics.

New media technology and public relations

One of the greater benefits of new media technologies is its impact on research and evaluation in the field of public relations. The advantages of, for example, online surveys, are the following:

- access to internal and external participants;
- the safe storage of results;
- computerised analyses;
- reduced cost; and
- real-time evaluation.

The online environment also enables easier management of:

- media lists;
- distribution of news releases;
- development and distribution of creative press kits (text, audio and video);
- advanced archive systems;
- tracking of publicity: online groups, web traffic, polls, etc;
- tracking of crisis situations: online updates, control room, enhanced communication with target publics, real-time FAQs through chat programmes; and
- geographically dispersed teams and online communities.

Summary

The Internet has changed almost everything about the way the information needed by the media is found, processed and managed. Public relations practitioners affiliated to companies and government institutions can now refer journalists to their websites for the latest copy of a news release, a report or a study. Journalists locate interview sources, both people and data, on the Internet. Interview sources often prefer first contact by e-mail, not telephone.

For better or for worse, the Internet has changed the process of newsgathering more profoundly and in a shorter period of time than any other development. As public relations practitioners we must be aware of this if we want to reach our target audience and build a bigger client base.

The Internet is definitely here to stay, but new resources and techniques are constantly being developed. As the Internet continues to gain momentum we must not be left behind. In professional and financial realms, those who do not have access to the latest in technological communication will find themselves at a distinct disadvantage.

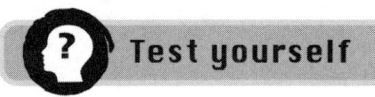

Test yourself

1. Explain your understanding of the term 'new media'.

2. Discuss how public relations practitioners can apply new media technology to improve their service.

3. Explain what you would need to be able to use the Internet.

4. Discuss the new media tool you can use to make your company known worldwide.

5. Your organisation is celebrating its centenary and you need to gather information relevant to the organisation for publication in your yearbook. Explain how you can use the different facets of the Internet to assist you.

6. Explain what e-mail means. Also, discuss how the public relations practitioner can apply this tool effectively when dealing with the mass-communication media.

7. Discuss how public relations practitioners can use social network sites such as *Twitter* and *Facebook* to gain favourable publicity.

Sources consulted

Employees of Media24, SABC and Texl 00.

Kelleher, T (2007) *Public Relations Online: Lasting Concepts for Changing Media*, California: SAGE.

Pitter, K (1998) *Every Student's Guide to Life on the Net*, USA: McGraw-Hill.

Turrow, S (1999) *Media Today — An Introduction to Mass Communication*, USA: Houghton-Mifflin Company.

How to use the various media

Objectives

After you have completed this chapter, you should be able to:

▶ analyse various newsworthy events in an organisation; and

▶ choose the most suitable media for these events.

Introduction

Thus far, you have been given a general idea of how newspapers, magazines, television and radio function. Besides the fact that a knowledge of these various media is imperative, the public relations practitioner should be able to analyse an event and decide which medium or media will publicise it most suitably.

Practical exercises

To assist you in the decision-making process, this chapter presents several scenarios. Analyse each one and, keeping in mind the types of media and their peculiar requirements, indicate the most appropriate medium for each scenario. Do not forget, however, that more than one medium might be suitable for some scenarios. In the case of the electronic media, indicate the category, then motivate your choice of media and category (where applicable).

We urge you to acquaint yourself with the various newspapers, magazines, radio services and programmes available in your area (suggested in the previous chapters). Familiarise yourself with the television programmes and categories available to you. By doing this, you will be able to give exact and real details when choosing media. Follow our advice. It will bring you closer to the real and exciting world of public relations.

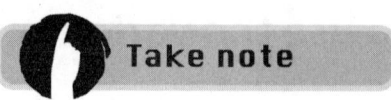

Take note

For each scenario, you must place yourself in the position of the organisation's public relations practitioner. These scenarios are possible newsworthy organisational happenings or events.

Scenario 1

The managing director of a large South African company (where you are employed as public relations practitioner) died in his office this morning after suffering a heart attack. He had headed the company for 15 years and was well known for the strong service he rendered the community during his term of office.

▶ *Choice of medium/media:* _____

_____

▶ *Category (if applicable):* _____

_____

▶ *Motivation:* _____

_____

Scenario 2

A strike by health workers has crippled patient services at a hospital in your area. Nurses have to stretcher patients in the absence of porters and deliver food trolleys to the various wards while volunteers prepare the patients' meals in the kitchen. As the laundry is not functioning, heaps of dirty linen are scattered around wards and the hospital grounds. Effective patient care cannot be rendered.

▶ *Choice of medium/media:* _____

_____

▶ *Category (if applicable):* _____

_____

▶ *Motivation:* _____

_____

_____

Scenario 3

The bank where you are employed is merging with another major financial institution. A change in corporate image and identity is planned.

▶ *Choice of medium/media:* _____

_____

▶ *Category (if applicable):* _____

_____

▶ *Motivation:* _____

_____

_____

Scenario 4

> You are the town municipality's public relations practitioner. The town is celebrating its centenary. Various events have been organised. They include:
>
> ▶ the freedom of the town to be conferred on President Jacob Zuma;
> ▶ a mass gymnastic event involving 100 surrounding schools; and
> ▶ a fete at the local sports grounds.
>
> ▶ Choice of medium/media: _____
> _____
>
> ▶ Category (if applicable): _____
> _____
>
> ▶ Motivation: _____
> _____

General exercise

> In the following exercise a list of news events is provided. Choose news events you consider appropriate for the following media:
>
> ▶ the local newspaper;
> ▶ a national newspaper;
> ▶ national and/or regional radio news bulletins;
> ▶ television news; and
> ▶ the Internet.

> An explosion at one of the company's plants seriously injures 10 employees.
>
> ▶ Media: _____

An organisational open-day where various activities for young and old have been arranged.

▶ Media: _____

A large investment in your company by a sister company abroad.

▶ Media: _____

Fraud involving millions of rand in the top ranks of your organisation.

▶ Media: _____

Your organisation's soccer team is to coach soccer players at local schools.

▶ Media: _____

Your managing director is killed during a robbery at your head office. The robbers escape with a large sum of money.

▶ Media: _____

To promote your organisatio's products/services worldwide.

▶ Media: _____

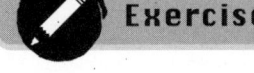 **Exercise**

CREATIVE THINKING!

Consider the list of events given in the general exercise. Think of articles that could be written about these events in magazines, eg a miraculous recovery by a victim involved in the explosion at the plant.

Summary

From these exercises the possibilities of the various media as well as the variety of issues a public relations practitioner has to face each day, become quite obvious. The creative public relations practitioner can turn many events into excellent opportunities to assure good media coverage.

ESSENTIAL JOURNALISTIC SKILLS FOR THE PUBLIC RELATIONS PRACTITIONER

A practical guide

The everyday responsibilities of a public relations practitioner include various tasks of a journalistic nature. These are not only directed at the media, but also include the application of journalistic skills in public relations where a knowledge of the basic principles of interviewing, photography, writing, design and page layout leads to a finer end result.

Public relations practitioners responsible for internal and external house publications could be considered 'internal' journalists or editors. These public relations practitioners also look for news, conduct interviews, take photographs, write and edit articles, and do page layout according to deadlines. Although the nature and content of internal and external house publications differ considerably from the mass-communication media, the basic principles stay the same.

Public relations practitioners are often inundated with tasks, eg designing invitation cards, compiling brochures and pamphlets, writing news releases, editing annual publications, etc. Basic journalistic skills will enable the public relations practitioner to maintain a high standard when doing these tasks.

This part of the book deals with the various journalistic skills public relations practitioners need in their everyday work. In chapter 2 we compared the skills of the public relations practitioner that overlap those applied by journalists. This section links with chapter 2, and in it we will discuss how these skills are applied by the public relations practitioner.

In part 3, we deal with the following journalistic skills applied by the public relations practitioner: interviews, photography, writing, editing and design (including page layout and desktop publishing).

Interviewing skills

After you have studied this chapter, you should be able to:

▶ conduct an interview (as a public relations practitioner);

▶ handle interviews by various journalists from different media; and

▶ apply general guidelines when dealing with the media.

Introduction

Mass communication media: technical channels used to convey messages to a large, diverse audience (general public), eg radio, television, newspapers, magazines, etc.

Interviewing is one of the journalistic skills the public relations practitioner will use frequently. The difference between journalistic interviewing and public relations interviewing is that the journalist has various external sources with whom interviews might be conducted. Those of public relations practitioners are limited and confined to their organisation since their main aim is to gather information for in-house publications. The public relations practitioner's chief sources are management, employees, former employees or pensioners and, sometimes, members of the community.

The other important fact is that the journalist's main aim is to gather information for publication or broadcast by media directed at a large and diverse body of receivers. The journalist is seldom interviewed by other journalists.

Journalists might be interviewed after being involved in or witnessing a newsworthy incident or when they uncover a spectacularly newsworthy story. This happened when a journalist from *Beeld* (a newspaper) broke the news that 'the Hunter baby' had been found two years after being kidnapped at birth. Because this was the kind of story that grabbed everybody's attention, the public was also keen to know how the journalist 'got the story'. Several interviews were conducted with the journalist.

Public relations practitioners, however, are well placed to interview sources and to be interviewed by journalists.

They therefore act as an *interviewer* and as an *interviewee* (respondent). They conduct interviews to gather information for in-house publications directed at a specific target group, eg employees. Journalists gather information for publication or broadcast through the mass-communication media, directed at the broad public.

Interviewer: a person conducting an investigative discussion

Interviewee: a person responding to a series of investigative questions

In this chapter, we focus on the public relations practitioners' application of interviewing skills and how they should handle journalists when being interviewed. General guidelines for dealing with the media are also discussed.

Interviewing

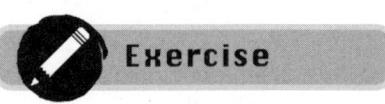 **Exercise**

Describe, in your own words, the term 'interviewing':

Compare your description with the following:

Interviewing is the gathering of information on a specific topic or person for the purpose of writing a news report, article, profile or feature for publication or broadcast.

The difference between an interviewer and an interviewee was described in the introduction.

Read through the introduction again and describe the difference between an interviewer and an interviewee.

In this chapter, interviewing should not be confused with discussions held to fill a vacant post. There is a big difference in the planning of and approach to an interview for publication or broadcast purposes and a job interview.

How to conduct interviews (as interviewer)

The public relations practitioner should know how to conduct interviews as a successful interview and its publication in an in-house publication can earn you credibility.

In the following discussion, we look at the practical aspects of arranging and conducting interviews.

To guide you in preparing for and conducting an interview, we use the following example.

A new managing director has been appointed at your organisation and you plan to interview him/her.

Factors to consider

Objective

Establish the aim of the interview. You must know beforehand what you want to achieve with the interview. The main objective is to introduce the new managing director to the target group.

Type of publication

Ask yourself this question. In which house publication will the interview be published? Since we differentiate between internal and external house magazines, you should know in which one the interview will be published. If you decide to publish it in both, this will lead you to another question.

Readers

Who are the readers of the internal/external house magazines? If the interview is published in the internal house magazine, the readers will comprise the organisation's present and past employees and perhaps their families. If the interview is published in the external house magazine, the readers include anybody outside the organisation, eg shareholders, community leaders, distributors and dealers, etc.

It is important to answer these questions, since the reason for the interview, the type of publication and the readers you are targeting will affect your preparation and the questions you will ask.

Preparing for the interview

You need to plan the interview before you can conduct it. It is important to gather as much information as possible about the new managing director before the interview. In the planning phase, you should attend to the 5Ws + 1H questions, ie Who, What, Where, When, Why and How? You can find answers to these questions in the following ways:

- Research is important. You should trace the MD's career back through other organisations. You might have to visit these organisations archives to get background information. You might also want to speak to the MD's former colleagues to gather more recent information.

  Background information helps you to become 'acquainted' with interviewees before you meet them. It also helps you in preparing a list of questions. Asking discerning questions about their background creates the impression that you are a professional public relations practitioner.

- Following on your research, you need to list several structured questions. Begin with light questions, move to more serious ones and then round off the interview. Keeping your objective, publication and readers in mind, you should ask questions that will realise your objective and interest your readers. Questions on issues such as the interviewees' career path, interests, ambitions, hobbies and family can assist in introducing them to your readers. Remember that your questions should be sensible.

Although a list of questions is a useful guide during an interview, you should allow yourself to deviate from your original questions. It often happens that an answer leads to a different line of questioning. This adds value to the planning you did before the interview.

Resources: a supply of tools that can be used

▶ Decide on the *resources* you will use during the interview. Will you write the answers in a notebook or will you record the interview? You may decide to use both methods. If you use a tape recorder, you must remember to ask permission from the interviewee (in this case, the managing director) to record the interview. Some people do not like to be recorded and you may therefore need their permission. It is advisable that you use one of these two resources as it is impossible to remember all that was said.

▶ Set a time for the interview. Although this may sound logical, it is a very important point. You can hardly expect the managing director to leave a meeting to grant you an unexpected interview. Setting a specific date and time for the interview will give the MD a chance to anticipate possible questions and to prepare answers. An appointment should be made through the managing director's secretary.

Do not volunteer a list of questions beforehand. You want spontaneous answers to add to the liveliness of the interview. However, if the MD insists on receiving a list of questions beforehand, you can hardly refuse.

Conducting the interview

The ideal would be to become acquainted with the managing director before setting up the interview. However, this is not always possible.

On arriving for the interview, introduce yourself in a friendly manner. Although you should be at ease, do not become familiar. Be professional at all times.

It is advisable to have an informal chat with the managing director before the interview. This will put him or her at ease. You can then begin your formal, prepared line of questioning. If you are using a tape recorder (with permission), turn it on and make sure that it records the whole interview.

If you are using a notebook, make short notes while writing down answers. If you do not have *shorthand* skills, it is suggested that you develop your own style of abbreviated writing. It is not possible to write answers down word for word — somewhere along the way you will find that you have lost words or sentences. This could result in a disastrous interview. Write down the answers' core words, which will enable you to restructure the interview properly afterwards.

Shorthand: a method of rapid writing in abbreviations and symbols

It is important to listen carefully to answers and to make sure that there is no misunderstanding. Rather ask an interviewee to repeat or rephrase an answer if you do not grasp the meaning of it. Also, if you are going to use direct quotations, you have to use the exact words. You cannot quote directly using your own words.

During an interview, it could happen that the person strays from the point. If this happens and you feel the information is irrelevant, gently steer him or her back to the point under discussion. You should control the interview.

If you are unsure of the correct spelling of the managing director's name and surname, ask him or her for it — do not be afraid to do so. You will be more embarrassed by a misspelled name or surname when the article is published than you will when asking for the correct spelling!

Remember to maintain eye contact during the interview (but do not stare!), smile or nod your head to show understanding, and look interested — it is up to you to make the interview a pleasant and rewarding experience.

Once you are satisfied that you have sufficient information, thank the interviewee for granting you the interview.

(These guidelines can be used for any interview.)

Your next step will be to write a profile. Refer to chapter 15 in which writing skills are discussed. You may also want to photograph the MD (with permission) during the interview. Chapters 14 and 15 will provide guidelines on taking appropriate photographs and writing a pertinent caption.

How to handle an interview (as interviewee)

We have dealt with the public relations practitioner as the interviewer. In this section, we discuss how the public relations practitioner should act when being interviewed, ie as the interviewee.

This section links to part 2 in which we discussed various media, ie newspapers, magazines, television and radio. You should therefore be aware of the differences between these media and their requirements.

A journalist may interview you on the telephone. However, he or she is more likely to choose to interview you at your office or, perhaps, at an agreed venue (depending on the reason for the interview).

We will use an example to guide you through the interview:

> *You are a public relations practitioner for a zoo where a baby chimpanzee's birth has caused great excitement. This is the first chimpanzee conceived* in vitro *in South Africa.*
>
> *Journalists from the different mass-communication media arrange to interview you on this event. You now have to prepare yourself for these interviews.*

Preparation

Anticipate the journalists' questions. Answers to the traditional 5W + 1H ones will be helpful. Who performed the procedure? Where and when was it performed? How was it done? Did the mother chimpanzee experience any difficulties during pregnancy or while giving birth? How much did the baby chimpanzee weigh at birth? Is it feeding from the mother? Answers to these questions will be important.

To find the answers, you will have to speak to the doctors involved in the procedure and those who attended the birth of the baby chimpanzee. You will also have to speak to the person tending it. Make notes of the information you have obtained as you will have to relay it to the journalist.

You should get permission and make arrangements for a photograph and other visual material of the mother and baby to be taken for the newspaper, magazine or television.

Remember, radio journalists will not need photographs, although they might wish to see them.

The interview

When the journalist arrives, make him or her feel welcome. Be relaxed when answering questions. Listen carefully to the question and only answer what is asked. Do not elaborate on issues unless the journalist requests more information. If a question is asked for which you do not have an answer, be honest and say that you will get the information. Do not try to ignore the question. Rather make a point of obtaining the information as soon as possible.

When the journalist is satisfied that sufficient information has been obtained, accompany him or her to the baby chimpanzee for the photographic or visual session.

Remember, each event and each situation might require different actions from you. The above is just an example of how you can prepare yourself for a successful interview.

Interviews with radio journalists are usually recorded. In the case of television, you will probably be interviewed 'on camera'. The best advice any interviewee can be given is to relax, relax, relax! If you are tense during the interview, the tension will be heard in your voice and will show on your face. The only way to learn to relax for interviews is to practise. Further hints and tips for a television interview are given later in this chapter.

Exercise

You will need a tape recorder, a video camera and a video playback facility to complete these two exercises.

Exercise 1

Take a specific event or happening at your organisation and prepare possible answers for an interview. Ask a colleague to act as a radio journalist (interviewer). The interview must be recorded. The journalist will ask you for a voice test to set the correct volume on the tape recorder. This will be played back and you may be asked to speak more loudly or softly, more slowly or faster. Once the journalist is satisfied, begin the interview.

On completing the interview, play it back and listen to it critically. Note the areas in which you need more exercise. Practise, practise, practise!

Exercise 2

You are now being interviewed by a television journalist. Your colleague has to use a video camera for this exercise. The difference here is that the interview is recorded immediately — there is no test run. When the interview is finished, use the video playback facility and analyse your appearance, facial expression, and the tone and pitch of your voice, etc. Once again, practise, practise, practise!

Remember: **practice makes perfect!**

Take note

If you do not have video facilities, practise in front of a mirror.

Tips for a television interview

▶ If the interview is going to take place at the television studio, you should allow the use of makeup on your face since the studio lights become very hot. Makeup will stop you from sweating excessively under the lights.

▶ Your appearance is very important. Always make sure that you dress neatly and comfortably. Television viewers often judge you on your appearance before you have uttered a word! You are representing your organisation — never allow anybody to think negatively of it because of your appearance. Also, choose clothes to which a lapel microphone can be attached.

▶ There are usually several cameras in the television studio. Do not look at them or at the activity around you — focus on the interviewer. It is not your concern if and when the camera focuses on you — your attention should be with the interviewer.

▶ Listen carefully to the questions and do not elaborate on an answer — airtime is limited.

▶ When a television journalist approaches you for an interview, ask whether you will be alone or whether you will be part of a panel discussion for a television programme. If you are a panellist, wait for the interviewer to address you before giving your answer. Do not interrupt others on the panel. If you feel that you would like to comment on another panellist's answer, indicate to the interviewer that you would like to speak. The interviewer is in control and you must abide by his or her decisions.

To acquaint yourself with the set-up of a radio or television studio, arrange a visit to the SABC. If you know how studios operate, you will feel more at ease when confronted by 'the real thing'.

Public relations practitioners should use their knowledge to prepare and assist members of management who are often in the interviewee's hot seat.

General tips for handling the media

In this section, a few tips are given that might assist you in dealing with the media.

- Never say 'No comment'. Whenever a journalist approaches you for a comment on an issue — especially sensitive ones — saying 'No comment' will take you nowhere. You should remember that the journalist already has a story that he or she will publish or broadcast. Rather take the opportunity to guide the journalist in objective reporting. You will be much more credible when giving information (even on sensitive issues).
- Do not give information you are not sure of. Rather tell the journalist that you need to verify the facts, then contact the journalist the moment you have them.
- Never promise to telephone back and then 'forget' to do so. This is bad manners. Even if you do not have the necessary information available, telephone the journalist and update him or her on your progress.
- Do not take any chances by giving information 'off the record'. Journalists thrive on information that you do not want to have published or broadcast.
- Never try to hide facts. The journalist's work is to dig for information. You will cause more damage in trying to hide facts and information than you will by being frank. Credibility is earned by being open and honest.

- Trust the journalist. Never ask him or her to fax you a copy of the news report or article before it is published or broadcast. Journalists abhor this. They work to tight deadlines and do not have the time to send information back and forth. Rather invite the journalist to contact you if he or she is unsure of any facts.

- Do not demand that the journalist tells you when the article, news report, etc. will be published or broadcast. The journalist does not control the publishing or broadcast of material. The final decision lies with others. It may happen that nothing is published or broadcast. Do not hold it against the journalist. Remember, there are many journalists covering many events and happenings throughout the day. If your story has more news value and is more important to the public than other stories of the day, you will get the publicity.

- Never become despondent after having spent many hours with a journalist only to find that you get no publicity. Your day will come. Act professionally at all times. Be helpful and polite, and never lose your temper.

- Always give the name and designation of the person acting as spokesperson, eg Dr Neil Barnard, heart surgeon at the Ga-Rankuwa Hospital; or Cathy Mokoena, public relations practitioner at Telkom, etc.

Take note

Remember, it is up to you. The journalist can be your greatest friend or your worst enemy!

Interview scenarios to consider

Consider the following scenarios (adapted from Shure, Burnett & Brown 2005:19–22):

Based on the premise that interviews may be scheduled for literally a few seconds, five minutes or longer, rather limit yourself to the three most important points that you want to make. These will become your 'islands of safety', which you will return to again and again during the interview.

Below are several scenarios which may arise when dealing with interviews. Consider the following:

What if the interviewer keeps moving away from the points I want to make?

Be polite, but firmly bring the interview back to the points you want to make by using 'bridges' beginning your answers by saying, 'Well, it means the real issues is …' and then state one of the points you want to make. Some of the following comments are useful 'bridges' you can use to make the points you want to make:

> Let me add…
> I'm often asked…
> That's not my area of expertise but I do know…
> It seems the most important issue is…

What if the reporter asks a question I do not want to answer?

Swim back to an 'island of safety'. Use a story to illustrate one of the three points you prepared in advance — people remember stories. Think of interviews you have listened to and you will probably remember a story that illustrated a point.

What if the reporter keeps interrupting me with questions?

Let the reporter interrupt. You may say, 'You've asked me several questions' and then answer the question you want to answer with one of your three points. If the interruptions are far from the points you were making and you want to get back, you may say. 'As I was saying…' and then continue your answer with one of your three points.

What if there is a long silence?

Stay silent. Do not volunteer unnecessary information. Do not be afraid of the silence. The interviewer is responsible for that time. In a slightly confrontational interview, silence is often a method that an interviewer may use to get a person to volunteer revealing information.

What if I am asked to add more or say more than I want to say?

Go back to your 'island of safety' — they are important enough to elaborate on and repeat, possibly with different stories or examples to illustrate the points.

What if I do not know the answer to a question?

Be honest. If you do not know the answer, say, 'I'm sorry, I don't have that information, but I'll be happy to get back to you with it'. When you say that, make sure you do get the information to the reporter.

How long should my answers be?

Your answers should be brief—approximately 20 seconds. However, they should be shorter for radio and longer for print.

What about how I look and sound (for television and radio)?

More than 90% of communication is non-verbal, so how you look and sound will be very important. Be enthusiastic and energetic. Both radio and television tend to 'flatten' people — ie make a person less exciting and more 'bland' — so be excited about what you are saying. It will be very helpful to videotape and review your practice session. You will probably find that you have to go past your 'comfort' point to show emotion when being interviewed for a television broadcast. If your interview is for television, you should follow some simple guidelines:

- wear solid colours — light but not white;
- do not wear flashy or shiny fabric;
- do not over-accessorise; and
- apply normal makeup and check it in the mirror before you go on air.

Can I say something to a reporter and expect it not to be used?

Never. Always assume the microphone or recorder is on. Many well-known people have been embarrassed by comments made when they thought the microphone was turned off. Assume that anything you say to a reporter at any time will be used and saying 'No comment' will usually give the impression that you have something to hide. A reporter is always working and there is no 'off the record' — unless you have reached explicit agreement on this point. Never say anything you do not want to read in print or hear on radio or television.

Summary

The public relations practitioner plays two roles in interviewing, ie as interviewer and as interviewee. As interviewer, skills are needed to conduct an interview for in-house publication purposes. As interviewee, the public relations practitioner gives information to journalists for publication in the mass-communication media. The correct handling of different media is of utmost importance in ensuring a successful interview.

The general hints and tips given for television interviewing and media handling should assist you when being confronted by 'the real thing'.

Test yourself

1. Explain, in your own words, what the term 'interviewing' means.

2. What is the difference between the interviewer and the interviewee?

3. List and discuss the three main factors you need to consider when planning to interview an employee at your organisation.

4. You need to prepare for an interview with an employee who is retiring after 30 years' service in the organisation. Detail how you, as the interviewer, will prepare and conduct the interview.

5. A journalist from a newspaper asks to interview you about employees striking at your organisation. Discuss in detail how you will prepare for and handle the interview.

6. A television journalist asks to interview you about the same strike. Discuss how you will prepare for and handle this interview.

Sources consulted

Clayton, J (1994) *Interviewing for Journalists*, London: Judy Piatkus Ltd.

Shure, S, Burnett, I & Brown, M (2005) *A Media Guidebook for Women: Finding Your Public Voice*, United States Agency for International Development (USAID).

Photographic skills

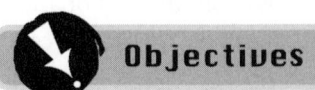

Objectives

After you have studied this chapter you should be able to:

▶ understand the basic features if a digital camera;

▶ recognise various organisational opportunities for photographs; and

▶ take better photographs.

Introduction

Digital cameras:
they capture images electronically rather than on film by an array of charge-coupled devices stored in the camera's random access memory or a special diskette and transferred to a computer for modification, long-term storage or printout

Photography is an invaluable and effective journalistic skill for the public relations practitioner. A knowledge of photography will enable the public relations practitioner to take photographs of organisational happenings and events for in-house publications. Including a good photograph will also add quality to press kits for publication in the print media.

Photography has gone through an exciting transition period during the last few years because of the new capabilities of *digital cameras*. The advantages of digital cameras over their analog counterparts are that the finished images can be reviewed immediately and erased, if necessary; one picture can be printed without waiting to develop an entire roll of film; and the storage mechanism most widely used for 'digital film' — the memory card — is reusable.

A basic knowledge of photography is essential for any public relations practitioner. In this chapter, basic guidelines are given on the technical aspects of digital cameras. Some practical advice is offered as we look at the advantages photographic skills hold for the public relations practitioner. At the end of the chapter, tips for taking photographs have been included.

The best way to acquire good photographic skills is to practice and to experiment with the camera, and to become acquainted with how it works and what it produces by setting up various scenes and taking photographs from various angles.

Those who are keen to become good at photography should take a course to acquire all the basic skills. Public relations practitioners should realise that photography is as important as any other communication tool, and should not be seen as the domain of the professionals. Knowledge of photography will not only enhance skills but will also help whenever it is necessary to use a professional photographer as exact needs should be communicated succesfully.

Features of a digital camera

The first step to becoming a good photographer is to become acquainted with the camera. There are many types of cameras available and the best way to learn how to operate one is to work through the instruction booklet that comes with it.

Digital camera features vary greatly from model to model. Some might be essential to a particular person, while others might be of use only for highly specialised applications.

Basic digital camera terms

Understanding the basic terms about digital cameras will enable users to have more control over a camera's features and will help them take the best-quality photos possible.

Megapixel (resolution)

The term 'megapixel' refers to the sharpness or detail of a picture. A million *pixels* make up a *megapixel* (MP). The higher the number of pixels, the higher the resolution. A camera that captures three million pixels, for example, is called a 3-megapixel camera.

Pixel: a contraction of the term 'picture element'. Digital images are made up of millions of tiny squares

165

A higher megapixel count means better-quality photos. Picture size is measured by how many pixels make up an image and this is done according to horizontal by vertical resolution, as in 1 280 × 960.

The resolution required will be determined by the purpose of the pictures.

Focal length (lens)

Focal length refers to how much the lens of a camera can magnify a shot, ie how much of a scene will fit into a picture. Some cameras have fixed focus lenses, which are preset to focus at a certain range. These pictures focus between a wide-angle lens and normal range. Many cameras have auto focus, which picks an item in the centre of the viewfinder around which to focus. To get an idea of a camera's range, it will be listed as the 35-mm equivalent.

Optical vs digital zoom

There are two types of zoom lens — digital and optical. Digital zoom enlarges the picture without adding any clarity of detail. It electronically enlarges the pixels in the centre area of a picture, meaning that any time the digital zoom function on a camera is used, the quality of the photograph is sacrificed.

Optical zoom uses the physical lenses inside the camera to enlarge a scene and will add detail and sharpness. Image quality stays high throughout the zoom range.

ISO

The term 'ISO' stands for 'International Standards Organisation', which sets standards for photography. The ISO range of a camera refers to how sensitive the camera is to light. For example, a low ISO number (100 or under) is not very sensitive to light and is best for shots in good lighting conditions. A higher ISO range means that the camera will be suitable for photography in darker conditions. It is best to look for a camera that has an adjustable range: ISO 100 to 400 should be adequate for most people's needs.

Shutter lag

Shutter lag refers to the time lag between pressing the button to take a photograph and the time when the picture actually gets taken. In general, with a digital camera, there is a 1–2-second time lag. Many camera manufacturers do not list the shutter lag time for their cameras, so the best way is to find this out by, testing a camera before buying it.

Memory

Digital cameras store pictures as data files. The size of the memory determines the number of pictures that can be taken before downloading them to a computer, at which time the memory can be filled up with new pictures. Most cameras come with only 8 megabytes (MB) of memory, which for a 2- or 3-megapixel camera could be only 10 to 40 photos. A removable memory, such as a memory card, may be purchased to provide more memory space.

Flash type

A flash is the extra light needed to shoot inside or in low-light conditions. Most digital cameras have built-in flashes. Other flash options include red eye reduction whereby two flashes are emitted. The first contracts the iris so that the eye reflects less light with the second flash. There is also the option of attaching an external flash that is much more powerful than the automatic flash.

LCD screen

An LCD screen shows what the photograph will look like and displays what has already been taken. It also allows the user to erase what is not needed.

Data transfer

Digital cameras come with a USB cable for transfer directly to the computer. Many computers have one or more memory card slots. Printers may also have card slots allowing photographs to be printed without using a computer. Wireless (wi-fi) transmission is also available on some cameras.

Battery duration

Digital cameras use either rechargeable or standard AA batteries. It can take an hour or more to recharge a battery — so having an extra, fully charged battery is recommended. AA batteries are readily available and rechargeable ones may also be used.

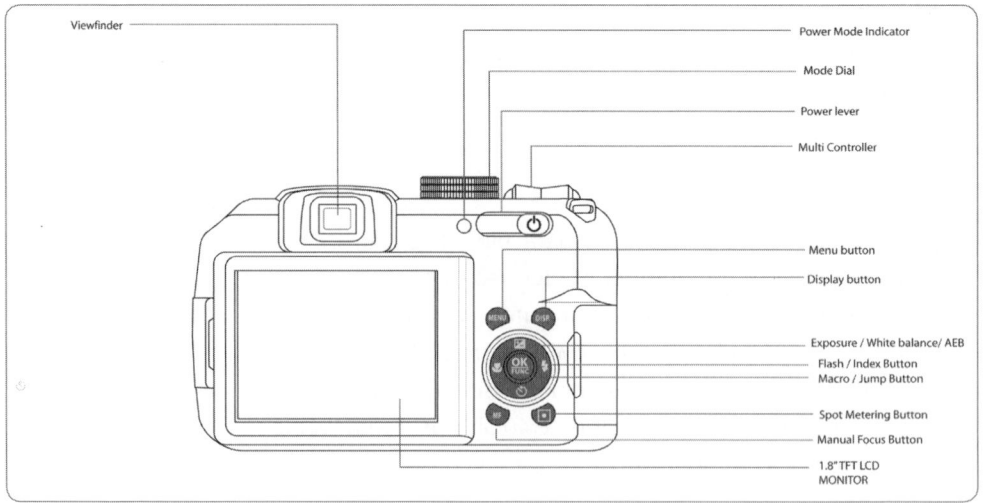

Figure 14.1. Basic parts of a digital camera

Other important photography terms

Composition

Composition is simply defined as the organisation of space within the photo. It is the combination of the subject matter within the photograph and its position in the picture scene. The position of the subject/s within the photograph can improve the way pictures look. Important factors to consider when composing a photograph are:

▶ the centre of interest;
▶ leading lines;
▶ balance; and
▶ contrast.

Exposure

Exposure refers to the amount of light required to produce an acceptable image when taking a photograph. Under-exposure means that there is too little light, resulting in dark undefined images. Over-exposure refers to too much light, resulting in images that have a poor resolution.

Aperture

The aperture is a hole of variable size inside a camera lens. The size of the aperture controls the quantity of light entering the camera.

Depth of field

The aperture controls the depth of field and field. Depth of field is the distinct focused area/zone in the photograph. The depth is how deep into the subject the distinct focus area/zone starts and ends.

Practical photography

Advantages of photography for public relations practitioners

Before we discuss aspects of good photography, it is necessary to establish the advantages of taking your own photographs. As the photographer, you need to create publicity and public relations pictures that do their intended job. As such, you must realise that publicity and public relations photographs do not revolve so much around a particular subject as they do around a particular purpose.

In-house publications

Public relations practitioners responsible for in-house publications can illustrate articles in the newsletter or magazine with photographs. It was mentioned in a previous chapter that you might want to take a photograph of the new managing director to accompany your feature story or profile. What better way of introducing the employees to their new managing director than with a photograph!

Furthermore, a good photograph can tell the reader more than words can describe. You should be familiar with the expression 'a picture paints a thousand words'. Here one can imagine, for example, a group of miners throwing their hardhats into the air, celebrating a million hours of accident-free shifts.

Certain organisational events, such as family-entertainment days can sometimes be best described by a photographic spread in the newsletter or magazine. Here the story is told by photographs and their captions.

Press kits

Most public relations practitioners will earn the admiration of journalists from the print media if their press kits contain photographs suitable for publication. Circumstances sometimes prohibit journalists from taking photographs. We can use the example of a child who has undergone a heart-lung transplant. Journalists are not allowed into the ward to take photographs because of the high risk to the child of infection. If you, as the public relations practitioner of the hospital, give the journalists a photograph, you will certainly be in their good books.

When including photographs with press kits, it is a good idea to make two or three different ones available so that journalists can choose those they wish to use. For example, the child who underwent the operation can be photographed alone, with her parents and with the doctor who performed the operation.

Photographs for press kits should be of a high quality for the print media. If the quality is in doubt, it is better either to leave them out or to hire a professional photographer to take some more.

Photographic library

Another advantage of public relations practitioners taking their own photographs is that they can establish their own photographic library with pictures of directors and managers, staff members or important organisational events. A photographic library can be extremely valuable if a photograph is needed urgently, for example, for a story in a newsletter about a staff member who has been promoted to a managerial post, but is presently overseas or if journalists need a photograph of the managing director. In such cases, photographs may be drawn from the files.

The photographic library of staff members should be updated every few years. It is a fact that we all change as we get older, whether we like it or not, therefore it is important to keep fairly recent photographs of staff.

Archives

Photographs can be of much archival value. The history of organisations is very important. If photographs of management and staff members who excelled are preserved together with photographs illustrating the organisation's growth and development, it will add great value to the archives.

Slide programmes

A further benefit for public relations practitioners who have a working knowledge of photography is that slide programmes can be made of the organisation's activities and staff members. These can be used for induction programmes or can be shown to people visiting or touring the organisation.

Displays/exhibitions

Most companies are given opportunities to take part in displays, exhibitions, etc where they can make use of good photographs to promote their company. Photographs from the archives or photographic library can be used for this purpose.

Now that we have established the advantages of taking your own photographs, we will look briefly at various photographic opportunities that may arise at organisations. We explore some ideas on the types of photographs that can be taken.

Photographic opportunities and types of photographs suitable for different occasions

The best way for public relations practitioners to take advantage of photographic opportunities is to know what is happening in their organisation. They should see to it that they are kept up to date with any departmental events or happenings that might create opportunities for good photographs. They should also be informed about staff members' activities. These activities should not be limited to work. Many staff members have interesting hobbies or are great sportspeople. Knowledge of their activities can broaden the public relations practitioner's ideas and range of plans for in-house publications well illustrated with good photographs.

The type of organisation will determine the type of photographic opportunities. We will therefore only give a limited overview of events that create photographic opportunities and the types of photograph that can be taken.

 **Take note**

Although we give some idea of the type of photograph that can be taken at these events, you should also be creative and take some candid shots, ie photographs taken of people without their being aware of you and who are therefore not posing.

> *Candid photographs can be extremely interesting and can enliven your publication. These 'natural' photographs often make much better material than posed photographs. They can also generate much fun — think of a photograph of the managing director's secretary taking a big bite from a slice of cream cake during a function!*

The following are events that create opportunities for photographs. Other events may be added to this list, such as crises or disasters at the organisation, etc.

Functions at the organisation

Almost every organisation holds various functions during the year. Examples include those to celebrate an organisation's centenary, the opening of a new plant, the naming of buildings or lecture halls, the inauguration of the new mayor, etc.

These functions create many opportunities for various types of photographs. Usually, dignitaries are present and photographs can be taken of them with the managing director. Photographs of a social nature can be taken, eg a group of staff having tea. It is surprising how many photographic opportunities arise during a function.

Awards ceremonies

These events, which are created in most organisations where staff members are awarded for their services, afford further opportunities. Faced with these ceremonies, one always tends to take photographs of the managing director presenting the staff member with the award. This is not wrong, but it is not very creative. An unusual alternative would be to take photographs of the award-winning staff member with a group of colleagues without whom he or she might not have excelled.

Management and staff members

Since an in-house publication should contain information about management and employees, photographs of the people concerned can support a story. The most common photograph one tends to take is the head-and-shoulders shot. Again, try something different. The reason for publishing a story about a staff member or manager is often an important issue or an achievement.

For example, a story of a staff member who makes porcelain dolls as a hobby could be well illustrated by a photograph of the person with some of the dolls.

If the story is more serious, eg an important policy change announced by the managing director, a photograph of the MD working at his or her desk is also a change from the traditional head-and-shoulders picture.

Sponsorships, donations or community projects

If an organisation involves itself in any type of sponsorships, donations or community projects, there are many photographic opportunities. For example, if the organisation sponsors the upliftment of community sport, a photograph could be taken of children being coached.

Open days, exhibitions and other public relations events

Open days and exhibitions are other events creating interesting photographic opportunities and public relations practitioners are responsible to keep abreast of events in their organisations offering photographic opportunities for in-house publications or other uses.

Exercise

List opportunities in your organisation for photographs suited to your newsletter.

Opportunities: _____

_____

Now describe the type of photograph you will take for each of the opportunities listed above.

Type of photograph: _____

_____

When planning photographs for an in-house publication, for press kits, etc, there are certain factors that need to be considered to ensure that you take good photographs. We discuss the most important factors.

Factors contributing to good photographs

Purpose of the photograph

One of the first questions you should ask yourself is whether you need the photograph. Why do you want to take a photograph of a certain person or event? Will it add to the quality or content of your publication?

It is important to answer these questions as photography is expensive. If you have good reason to take a photograph, you should ask yourself what the photograph is going to 'say' to your readers. This brings us to the next factor.

The relevance to the content of your article

Keep your message in mind at all times! When you use a photograph with a story or article, make sure that the photograph is relevant to its content. Remember, a photograph is used to support the content and must not contradict it. Exclude everything from the photograph that does not help to convey the message.

People

It is very important that your photograph 'lives'. Make use of people in your photographs. For example, if you take a photograph at an exhibition, get somebody to pose with the exhibit. Never take a photograph of 'dead' objects as such photographs are not very interesting to readers.

Background

Always make sure that you have a good background for your photograph. Poor backgrounds lead to poor photography. Often you may have only one chance to take a specific picture and it is therefore important that you do not spoil a good photograph with a poor background. Look for intrusive objects such as lights hanging from a ceiling above the subject's head or other people in the background. Be on the lookout for anything that may distract the reader's attention from the person or group you are photographing.

Figure 14.2 example of a poor photograph (note the funny 'hat' on head of the woman in the middle.)

In some instances, however, backgrounds may add to the impact of the photograph. Here we think of a photograph taken of a manager with the relevant company's logo or name in the background.

Space

When you take a photograph, make sure that the subject is centred. If you are composing a group photograph, always ask your subjects to stand close together. Do not take photographs with large spaces or gaps between people.

Clarity

When you take a photograph of a single person, do not stand too far away from the subject because his or her face might not be recognisable. The same principle applies to group photographs. Rather choose five people from the group for your photograph than taking a picture of 15 people who will not be recognised because of the distance.

Framing photographs

Always make sure the person you are photographing is well framed. In other words, make sure that you have full sight of the subject on the camera's LCD screen. If you take a head-and-shoulders portrait, make your cut-off point at the collar bone and not under the chin. When you take a full-length picture, make sure that the feet are also in the frame. If you want to get closer but still need depth, frame the subject from the waist upwards.

Take note

Always remember that your photograph can be edited afterwards, but that editing cannot correct what is not there.

Figure 14.3 This picture would portray more detail if taken from the waist upwards

Use the highest resolution that the camera offers. This will prevent or minimise the need for cropping in post-editing and ensures the retention of digital information required to produce and improve the image.

Facial expressions

Make sure that facial expressions suit the event. If you are taking a photograph of someone who has lost a relative, a smiling face is not appropriate.

Faces should not be turned away from the camera and the subject or subjects must look at the camera. Readers will not be interested in their backs or the backs of their heads.

Horizontal and vertical photographs (landscape and portrait)

One sometimes only wants to take a photograph with the camera in a horizontal position (landscape), often trying to squeeze the subject into the horizontal frame. If you have problems in getting a good landscape photograph, turn your camera to the vertical position (portrait). This may solve your problem.

You need to take a photograph of a staff member who was chosen as a member of the athletics team for the Olympic Games. Describe how you will plan the photograph, give an indication of its content and detail the factors you will consider when setting up the portrait.

General tips

▶ Know your camera. Read the manual and purchase a book on the basics of digital photography — look at photography magazines and magazines in your industry to see the images other people produce.

▶ Let there be light. Digital cameras are far more light tolerant the their film counterparts. Nevertheless, understanding light and how to control it is vital in creating the best pictures. Correct lighting — natural or artificial — is essential to achieve good colour rendition, contrast and the light and shade that create depth and interest.

▶ Steady the camera. Some cameras compensate for hand wobble but it is still better to have pin-sharp images from the outset. You can steady the camera against a solid object or use a tripod.

▶ If you are taking a photograph outdoors, in the middle of the day, you will find that the faces of the people you are photographing might be marred by shadows. Using a flash to light such shadowing will remove most of it from their faces. This is also a good technique to use when there is too much backlighting in your photograph.

- ▶ Carry spare memory cards in case you need more storage.
- ▶ Transfer and backup your images. Get them off the camera and onto more permanent storage systems as soon as possible. Remember to create a backup copy. When editing digital images, always use a copy of the image and never the original. You can re-edit images in many ways so do not destroy your originals.
- ▶ Test print. Produce a test print on your printer before sending an image or file to an editor.

Things you should never do

- ▶ Do not expect an expensive camera to make you a professional. If you know what you are doing, an inexpensive camera will produce better results than the most expensive camera in the hands of someone without a clue. Digital pictures still need creative inspiration, carefully considered exposure, framing and composition.
- ▶ Do not rely exessively on digital post-editing, which can be costly and time consuming. Get the best image you can from the outset.
- ▶ Do not use a cellphone camera for public relations photographs.
- ▶ Do not forget to back up.
- ▶ Do not panic. The more you use your digital camera, the better you will become and the more fun it will be.

Summary

In this chapter, guidelines are given to enable you to understand the basic features of digital cameras.

Public relations practitioners will benefit by taking their own photographs for use in in-house publications, press kits, etc.

Public relations practitioners should inform themselves of organisational events that create photographic opportunities, eg functions, awards ceremonies, etc.

Although you may have a very good camera, a photograph will only be as good as your control of the camera. When taking photographs, cognisance must be taken of relevance, background, people, space, etc.

? Test yourself

1. Discuss the basic features of a digital camera.

2. List the advantages of photography for a public relations practitioner who has a knowledge of it.

3. The organisation's involvement in community projects affords photographic opportunities. Identify a community project with which your organisation is involved and describe the photographs you intend taking.

4. List and discuss factors you need to consider when you want to take good photographs.

5. Snow has fallen in Johannesburg for the first time in 20 years. During lunchtime, some staff members decide to build a snowman and they ask you to take a photograph. You are faced with a very white background. How will you overcome this problem and ensure that your photograph is not overexposed?

Sources consulted

Daye, D (1994) *35mm Camera Handbook*, England: Bison Books Ltd.

Hausman, C & Benoit, P (1990) *Positive Public Relations*, USA: Liberty Hall Press.

http://www.abbysguide.com

http://www.basic-digital-photography.com

http://www.encyclopedia2-thefreedictionary.com

http://www.free-pr-advise.co.uk

http://www.wikipedia.org

Writing skills

After you have studied this chapter, you should be able to:

▶ explain why basic writing skills are important for the public relations practitioner;

▶ identify and describe the various types of article often written by public relations practitioners;

▶ write a news release and feature article; and

▶ write captions, headlines, etc.

Introduction

Annual report: a report containing important information about the company's past year, circulated among interested parties

Public relations practitioners in most organisations are responsible for a considerable amount of written material, from *annual reports* to internal newsletters, to invitations and news releases. Apart from writing most of this material, they often have to edit and approve many other documents written for different purposes by other staff members.

This can be a heavy burden as the image of any company is, to a great extent, dependent on such printed matter. A typing error on an invitation card could create a negative perception if you send such an invitation or it could result in a complete and costly reprint.

Apart from writing or editing written material, the public relations practitioner often has to make decisions about the final layout of organisational publications. This function is important and is dealt with in chapter 16.

Writing skills needed by public relations practitioners

Although not all public relations practitioners are born writers, a natural talent for writing is invaluable. It is unthinkable not to have a proper command of language and grammar. Computerised spelling checks and other means of checking language and word choice can eliminate unnecessary mistakes, but should not be totally relied upon.

Although public relations is a very different profession to journalism, public relations practitioners can learn a lot about writing from journalists. Even though journalists, especially news reporters, tend to write anything and everything according to the '5Ws + 1 H', nicely fitted into an inverted pyramid structure, they never bore readers with unnecessary and unimportant detail.

Public relations practitioners need not write according to a news-paper style but, in certain circumstances, doing so could be used to their advantage. Using this formula, facts about organisational change, new policies, procedures, etc can be arrestingly written. But what do public relations practitioners have to write most often? What is expected of them and how do they approach different issues? Let us look at the public relations practitioner's most common writing responsibilities.

News releases

What is a news release?

A news release, also known as a media or press release, is a written document designed to deliver a newsworthy message to the media, usually with the purpose of generating publicity about an organisation or event.

Sending a news release by mail, fax or e-mail is one of the most common methods a public relations practitioner uses to liaise with the media. It is worthwhile remembering that a news release should be well focused and have enough news value to be turned into a news report.

Take note

The public relations practitioner should also remember that different media need different information and that each news release should be written and presented according to the specific needs of a medium. While radio does not need pictures, pictures aimed at the community can be included in local community newspapers. Different pictures should be sent to different publications.

Structure of a news release

News releases are usually structured in the same manner as standard newspaper articles. The information is presented in an inverted pyramid, descending in a logical manner, from the most important to the least important. The inverted pyramid writing style assists the public relations practitioner in getting the most important message across to the media.

Inverted pyramid

The inverted pyramid method is still widely used today by journalists, the media and by public relations practitioners. It is a popular method because it tells readers quickly what they need to know.

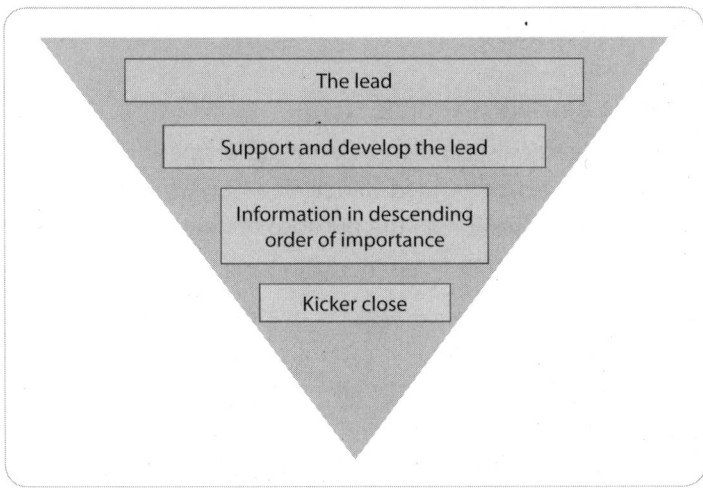

Figure 15.1 The inverted pyramid method of writing (Nel, F 1994:52)

According to Botha *et al* (2007:139–140), the key elements in the inverted pyramid structure can be described as follows:

The lead

The first paragraph of a story is called the lead paragraph. This generally consists of new factual information that is the most important or the most interesting. The lead paragraph is therefore a critical paragraph. This paragraph must explain the 5Ws + 1H (Who, What, When, Where, Why and How) and should get your audience interested in reading more of the story. The next paragraph should develop the story in more detail.

Support and develop the lead

Include any other important facts and information to support the facts provided in the first paragraph. Background information or quotes from credible sources can also be included in this paragraph.

Information in descending order of importance

Other information of lesser importance can be included in this paragraph or in subsequent paragraphs.

Closing with a kick

François Nel (2005) maintains that although an inverted pyramid story assumes the end of the story is the least important and can, if necessary be cut, the ending need not be dull. Editors are becoming more sensitive to writing and will often work to cut other parts of the story, if length is a consideration, in order to keep a good ending. Closing with a kick can turn the inverted pyramid format into a champagne glass structure, in which additional important information is imparted at the end.

Writing styles

One of the easiest ways of learning to write a news release is to study newspaper articles and to see how news stories are written. The most common writing styles are the 5Ws + 1H; SOLAADS and NIBSS.

5Ws + 1H

The 5Ws + 1H model of writing is a quick method for identifying the most important aspects in your story. For example, when writing your news release, ask yourself the questions: Who?, What?, When?, Where?, Why? and How?. Figure 15.2 illustrates this writing model.

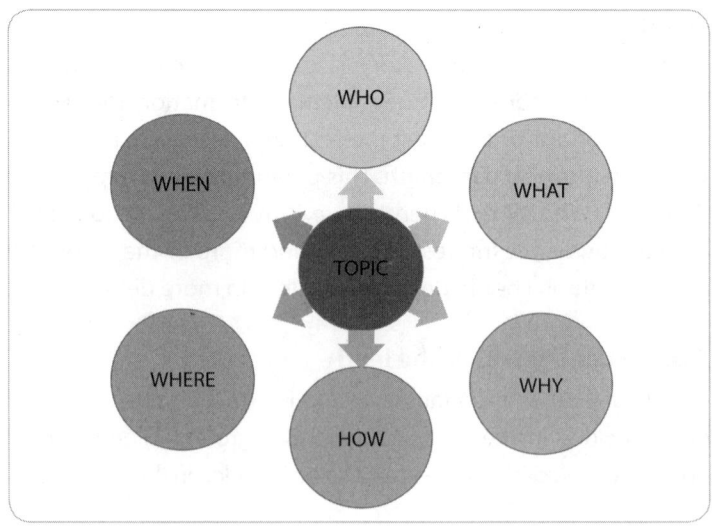

Figure 15.2 The 5Ws + 1H writing model

SOLAADS

Another good writing style is the SOLAADS method proposed by public relations guru Frank Jefkins. Jefkins' (1994) formula is:

- **S**ubject — What is the story about?
- **O**rganisation — What is the name of the organisation?
- **L**ocation — Where is the organisation located?
- **A**dvantages — What is new? What are the benefits? What does the reader want/need to know?
- **A**pplications — What are the uses? Who are the users?
- **D**etails — What are the sizes, colours, prices, performance figures, distributors?
- **S**ource — What/who is the source of the information and where can the journalist go to get more information or get clarification? It is most important to put in direct-line phone numbers and cellphone numbers.

NIBSS

Public relations practitioner Ralph Cohen (2007) suggests the NIBSS formula for selecting material for inclusion in a news release. NIBSS stands for:

- **N** = New information — this is the hard news.
- **I** = Interesting facts — this can be hard news, but more interesting.
- **B** = Background — this is putting the story in perspective and providing details about the company/event.

- **S** = Selling points — this is used especially for product releases to alert potential buyers to unique selling points.
- **S** = Superfluities — material that can be cut by the editor with no loss of meaning.

News release: example

The news release has a specific structure and format. While its style may vary from one organisation to another, a standard format can be used. Figure 15.3 shows a standard example of a news release:

Media release

Full date line

Wednesday, 21 July 2010

FOR IMMEDIATE RELEASE

Include this label.

NEW BOOK ON SOUTH AFRICA IS A MUST-HAVE!

Headline – in **BOLD, CAPS**

Co-founder of the 'Awesome SA' movement and self-confessed South Africa 'addict', Derryn Campbell, has written and produced an innovative, informative and entertaining new book on South Africa, called 'Awesome South Africa'. This colourful, 224-page collection is jam-packed with stories, facts, figures, anecdotes, graphics and photographs, offering an eclectic and informative insight into all that is South African.

Lead – answer the 5Ws and H

After leaving behind a successful corporate career in management, Derryn followed a vision to encourage South Africans to positively influence the future of their country. This passion led to her co-founding 'Awesome SA', a non-profit movement that not only interacts with South Africans to create awareness about their country, but also facilitates initiatives to deliver positive outcomes.

The preceding paragraphs follow the inverted pyramid style of writing.

'Awesome South Africa' is a visual cacophony of unique, exceptional and noteworthy things about South Africa, its heritage, its people and its heart. Irrespective of age, race or gender, the book is sure to be enjoyed by everyone – cynic and enthusiast alike.

A read of it will intrigue you, make you laugh, astonish and astound you.

Packed full of information, colourful graphics and photographs, this entertaining compilation contains interesting facts and trivia about the country and its people. If you are a South African, this book is guaranteed to stir feelings of pride, patriotism and belonging. If you are not, then it will leave you in awe and give you a comprehensive overview of this unique and crazy country.

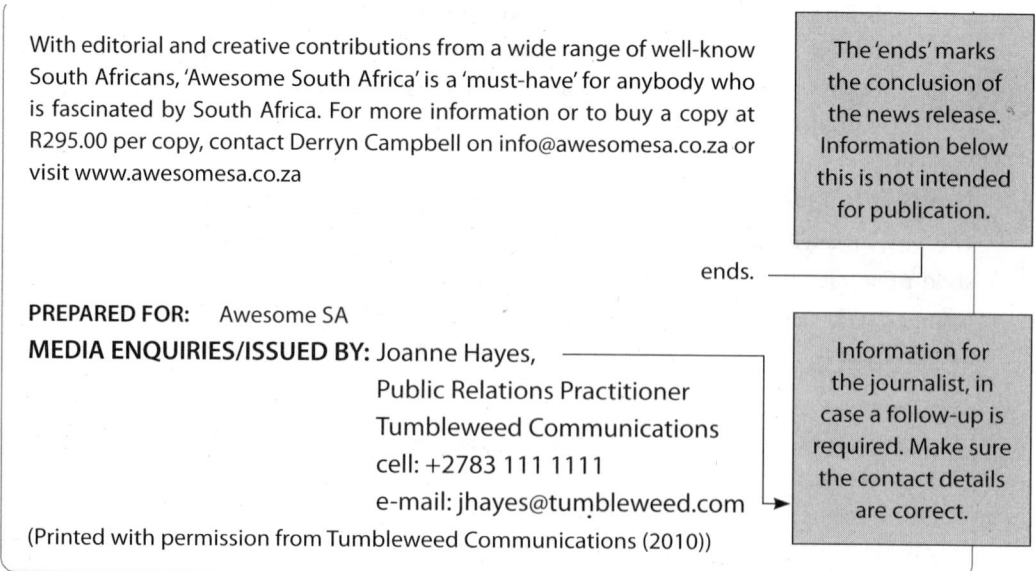

With editorial and creative contributions from a wide range of well-know South Africans, 'Awesome South Africa' is a 'must-have' for anybody who is fascinated by South Africa. For more information or to buy a copy at R295.00 per copy, contact Derryn Campbell on info@awesomesa.co.za or visit www.awesomesa.co.za

> The 'ends' marks the conclusion of the news release. Information below this is not intended for publication.

ends.

PREPARED FOR: Awesome SA
MEDIA ENQUIRIES/ISSUED BY: Joanne Hayes,
Public Relations Practitioner
Tumbleweed Communications
cell: +2783 111 1111
e-mail: jhayes@tumbleweed.com

> Information for the journalist, in case a follow-up is required. Make sure the contact details are correct.

(Printed with permission from Tumbleweed Communications (2010))

Figure 15.3 Example of a media release

Writing tips

▶ Remember that your news release MUST contain newsworthy information to attract the attention of the media. Avoid writing the news release like an advertisement as this destroys the validity of the news story.

▶ Use short paragraphs and keep your sentences simple.

▶ Aim for brevity; your news release should not be very long as journalists' time is limited.

▶ Avoid using jargon and language that encourages cynicism in journalists, such as 'the best' and 'world famous'. It is best to aim for an impartial, unbiased tone.

▶ Include a quote from a source related to the story, but only if the quote is original and adds value to the news release.

▶ Proofread and spell check your news release carefully. You will lose credibility if your press release is littered with spelling and grammatical errors.

▶ Avoid using the same news release for all journalists. Try to write different versions of the news release for different media publications, for example, a local newspaper and a national newspaper. For radio, keep your news release short — between 60 and 100 words.

▶ The headline or the heading of the news release should grab the attention of the editor. It should summarise the main ideas of the news release, but in a way that is exciting and dynamic. Remember you have just a few words to make your release stand out among the many others editors receive. It should always be in capital letters.

> Subheadings are generally unnecessary and should be avoided.

Using the above news release example, see how the journalist used it in the published newspaper report:

GET IT (Highway, Berea)
01 Jun 2010
Page : 4 #

Awesome South Africa
Co-founder of Awesome SA and self-confessed South African addict, Derryn Campbell's innovative, informative and entertaining book on South Africa, entitled *Awesome South Africa* is a must-have for your bookshelf. This colourful 224-page collection is jam-packed with stories, facts, figures, anecdotes, graphics and photographs, offering an eclectic and informative insight into all that is South African. Retails at R295. Contact Derryn Campbell on info@ awesomesa.co.za or visit www.awesomesa.co.za

Figure 15.4 The final newspaper report based on the information in figure 15.3

Features

Features can be described as any editorial content other than news — material containing advice, comment, opinion, assessment or subjective as opposed to objective news material (Hodgson 1993:264).

Features, also referred to as soft news, differ from news reports as they are not written according to the inverted pyramid structure, and the same emphasis is not put on the 5Ws +1 H. They are not time sensitive like the hard-news story and allow the writer time to do in-depth research on the subject matter and therefore provide the reader with more detailed information. Features therefore tend to be longer than news reports.

Features do not have a standard structure, allowing the writer greater freedom. Their style is informal and they often start with a quote or by creating an atmosphere. There are different types of features, each serving a particular purpose.

Types of features

News features

News features often appear in newspapers and focus on interesting or important background information relevant to topical news or issues. They are often written by experienced journalists and are usually situated on the page adjacent to the 'editorial comment' page. Regular columns, depending on their content, can also often be considered feature articles.

Personality profiles

The personality profile is one of the most popular forms of human interest features. Personality profiles are written to bring an audience closer to a person. Interviews and observations, as well as creative writing are used to paint a vivid picture of the person.

> **Example**
>
> *Dressed in a tan suit and sporting huge gold rings on each little finger, Benni McCarthy occasionally flashed his electrifying feel-good smile to the ladies waiting for autographs.* Each phrase reveals something about Benni's personality.

Human interest stories

A human interest story is written to show a subject's oddity, or emotional or entertainment value. Human interest stories can be tragic, uplifting or simply bizarre.

Trend stories

A trend story examines people, things or organisations that are having an impact on society. People are interested in reading or hearing about the latest fads and trends that makes such stories popular. Examples could include the latest fashion trends, a new religion or an increase in hijackings.

In-depth stories

An in-depth story provides a detailed account well beyond a basic news story or feature. It can be a lengthy news feature thatexamines one topic extensively such as an investigative story that reveals wrongdoing by a person, agency or institution. An example could be a story that exposes corruption and fraud by a government official.

Backgrounders

A backgrounder (analysis piece) adds meaning to current issues in the news by explaining them further. These stories bring an audience up to date, explaining how a country, organisation, person or situation got to be where it is now.

Writing and organising features

Feature writers seldom use the traditional inverted pyramid form; instead they may write chronologically and build the story up to a climax at the end. Their stories are held together by a thread, and they often end where the lead started. Although there is no standard structure to follow when writing a feature, there are guidelines that may assist the writer in drafting the feature.

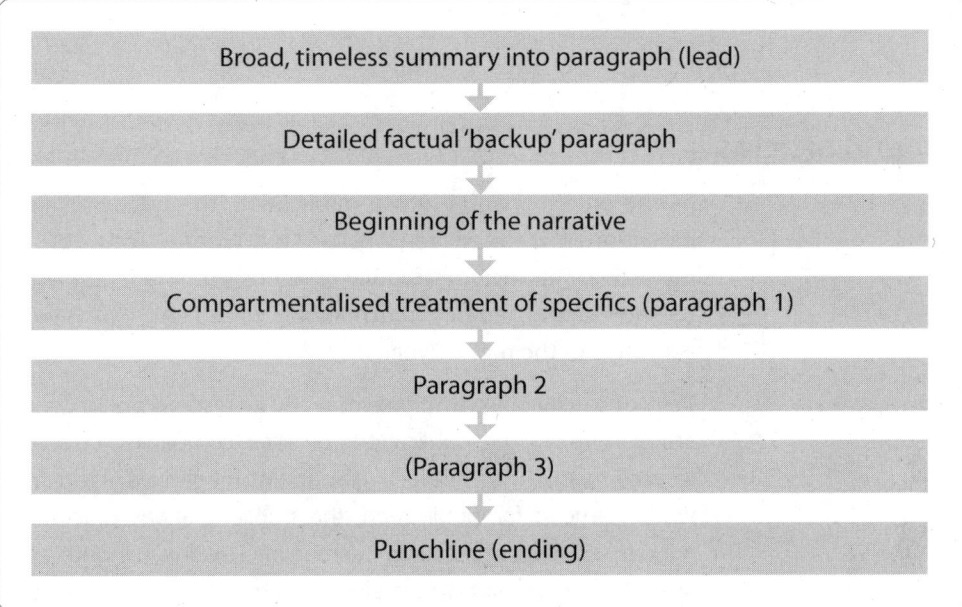

Figure 15.5 Guidelines for drafting a feature

The lead pulls together pieces of a developing puzzle or spotlights a trend. A detailed backup paragraph or two support the lead and gives evidence of the trend or development already highlighted in the lead. Thereafter, the story may be told in chronological order or in descending order of importance.

The ending is very important in feature stories; unlike with the inverted pyramid of the news report, the feature must end with some impact. Depending on the type of story, it can end with a quote or a 'moral of the story' statement or even a joke.

Tips for writing features

▶ Pick a theme.
▶ Write a captivating lead.
▶ Provide vital background information.
▶ Use clear, concise sentences.
▶ Use a thread to connect the different elements of the feature.
▶ Use transitional words to tie the paragraphs together.
▶ Conclude with a 'bang'.

Write a personal profile of yourself.

General articles

As the editor of an in-house publication, the public relations practitioner is often responsible for writing most of the magazine. This includes regular columns, comments on letters to the editor, general information, 'what's on', 'who's who', achievers of the month/year, etc.

The public relations practitioner may also be responsible for general articles used in the publications of sister companies, or articles to accompany news releases to specialist magazines. Apart from writing articles for publication, the public relations practitioner may also be responsible for generating information in monthly and annual reports, reports to shareholders, etc.

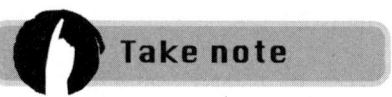

When writing any article, care should be taken to use good language, keep to the subject, avoid providing unnecessary information and, above all, to avoid using too many adjectives. Adjectives can easily frustrate the intelligent reader.

Light stories

Readers always appreciate a piece written in a lighter vein, provided it is tasteful and aimed at the right market. In-house publications can be brightened by a regular cartoon strip or a cartoon character making humorous comments on relevant issues. However, great care should be taken with light stories as some people might feel offended by them. They should always be in good taste and should never insult readers.

Captions

Information accompanying a photograph is called a caption, and its purpose is to add information. Photographs should not be used without captions.

Captions differ and are written for different reasons. They are often written for photographs accompanying an article or news report. In other cases, the photograph is not accompanied by an article or story. The caption has, therefore, to be written in such a way that it tells the story.

A caption for a group photograph of a new hockey team that accompanies an article should tell the reader who the team members are. Such captions are called identifiers.

In other situations, photographs may need supporting information, eg a photograph of a bereaved family. The family members appearing in the photograph must be identified, and information must be given about the deceased and the circumstances in which he or she died. This kind of caption is sometimes referred to as a self-contained caption.

When a photograph is not accompanied by an article or report, its caption story should include more information than usual and will, therefore, be longer. For example:

At a computer workshop in the conference centre, curious staff members listen to the advantages of the computer program that will, next month, replace the existing program. The workshop, presented by computer fundis, was organised after staff aired their concerns about the change.

Let us look at guidelines for caption writing:

- Remember, the main aim of a caption is to add additional information to a photograph.
- Never state the obvious, ie that which is clearly visible in the photograph.
- Always write the first and surnames (as far as possible) of people in photographs, and their designation where applicable, eg Mr Toni Jones, managing director of Gold Fields South Africa (GFSA).
- Keep the purpose of the photograph in mind. You may wish to create an atmosphere of excitement, sadness, etc. Think of your caption story as a small introductory paragraph. Answer the 5Ws + 1H in three to four accurate, concise lines. When you write a 'caption story' for a photograph, try answering the most important 5Ws + 1H questions. Remember, there is no other copy accompanying the photograph.
- Do not refer to the photograph using phrases such as 'Here you see ...', etc.
- Captions will be influenced by the story accompanying a photograph. If the financial director comments on the budget, and a head-and-shoulders photograph is used, a very short identifying caption is sufficient. A short quote could also be used effectively.
- A good caption can enhance a fair photograph, but a bad caption can ruin a great one.
- Be meticulous about spelling names. It is extremely unprofessional to use a misspelled or incorrect name.
- Write your caption in the present tense, whenever possible.

Exercise

Cut out five photographs with their captions. Evaluate these captions according to the guidelines we have just discussed.

Cut out five photographs without their captions. Build your own story around the photograph and write a 'caption story' for each.

Photographic pages

Photographic pages or 'spreads' are an easy way to fill pages in a publication when news is scarce. Subjects or topics on which to build a photographic page are not hard to find and can include almost anything. Think of any recent developments, social functions, promotions, a sports day, etc. Each could provide enough photographic material to design a photographic page.

Every picture on the photographic page should have a caption — unless different pictures are used to illustrate something and need no explanation. Information might be given in a separate information block, called a blurb.

A popular approach to photographic pages is to use a headline, an information block (blurb) to provide the necessary information, and a variety of photographs of different sizes and shapes with captions to tell the story.

Exercise

Compile a photographic page of yourself with at least eight photographs. Write a caption for each photograph and organise them so that they tell the story of your life.

Headlines

Writing headlines is not easy and is normally done during the sub-editing process by subeditors with many years' experience. However, this should not stop the public relations practitioner from writing creative headlines to enliven articles.

Apart from headlines for in-house publications, the public relations practitioner may often be responsible for writing headlines for other purposes. How should this task be approached? The following guidelines should put you on the right track.

- A headline should fit the available space.
- Headlines attract attention. They must be brisk and attractive.
- Headlines must provide just enough information to make a reader curious. If it provides all the important information, the reader will not read the article.

- Headlines should be short and to the point.
- Present and future tenses must be used to create a feeling of relevance and newsworthiness.
- One-word headlines are acceptable but should not be used too often, eg 'Victory' when South Africa wins a World Cup.
- Headlines can be supported above or below by subheadings.
- Use verbs in headlines in the active rather than the passive voice, eg 'Bafana Bafana win African Cup' is better than 'African Cup won by Bafana Bafana'.
- Do not use 'he' or 'she' in headlines. Rather: 'Postman saves drowning girl' or 'Robbers attack mother and baby'.

Apart from these guidelines regarding the content of headlines, the physical appearance is just as important. Guidelines on physical appearance are followed by the layout artist according to the style rules of the publication, and include aspects such as size, typeface, fonts, right and left alignment, etc.

Keep in mind that the two main functions of a headline are to draw the reader's attention to the story and to form part of the visual pattern of the newspaper page. (The latter is the task of the layout artist.)

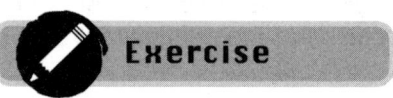

Exercise

Cut out five news reports without *their headlines. Read the content carefully and write your own headlines.*

Cut out five news headlines and evaluate them according to the guidelines given above.

Summary

From the discussion in this chapter, it should be clear that a public relations practitioner has important writing responsibilities. Errors must be avoided at all costs as one cannot correct a mistake after publication.

Test yourself

1. List the different types of writing tasks public relations practitioners are often required to do.

2. Explain what you understand by the term 'feature' and describe the different types of feature articles.

3. What are light stories? How will you use them in your publication?

4. Describe different types of captions and give examples of each.

5. What does the term 'photographic page' mean to you?

6. Briefly discuss the requirements of and the guidelines for writing headlines.

7. Identify the different writing styles that can be used to structure your news release.

8. Explain how the inverted pyramid structure is used to help you organise your news release.

9. Draft a news release using an appropriate style and format.

Sources consulted

Botha, D, Chaka, M, Du Plessis, N, Krause, B, Rawjee, VP, Porthen, D, Veerasamy D & Wright, B (2007) *Public Relations: Fresh Perspectives*. Cape Town: Pearson Education South Africa.

Cohen, R (2007) *Press Release Writing Tips. 39 tips by Professor Ralph Cohen*. Available at: http://press-release-writing.com/resources/writers.htm [Accessed on: 2 August 2010]

Hodgson, FW (1993) *Subediting — A Handbook of Modern Newspaper Editing and Production* (2 ed) Great Britain: Redwood Books.

Jefkins, F (1994) *Public Relations Techniques*, London: Butterworth-Heinemann.

Nel, F (1994) *Writing for the Media*, Cape Town: International Thomson Publishing Southern Africa.

Nel, F (2005) *Writing for the Media in Southern Africa* (3 ed), Cape Town: Oxford University Press.

CHAPTER
16

Design and page layout

Objectives

After you have studied this chapter, you should be able to:

▶ edit copy and photographs;
▶ do basic page layout by hand;
▶ write and fit headlines; and
▶ have a fair idea of what desktop publishing entails.

What this chapter is all about

Editing: assembling, preparing, modifying or condensing copy

Design: the process of using different options to lay out or design a page

Page layout: the way in which printed matter is set out

Editing and *design* skills are of great value to public relations practitioners. A basic grasp of these skills not only gives you an edge when it comes to making final decisions on a publication, it also enables you to work according to set guidelines.

Responsibility for a publication encompasses the successful management of a range of endeavours. The result does not only reflect the degree of success achieved in these endeavours, it illustrates how the publishing process has been managed throughout.

In this chapter, we look first at what editing involves and then we focus on basic design and *page layout*. You may question the importance of manual editing and page layout when computers have become increasingly adept at fulfilling these tasks. The answer is simple. A computer needs an operator. The operator responsible for page layout needs knowledge of design and layout principles and the skills to manipulate the computer program.

A basic knowledge of page layout — the kind of knowledge that will guide you to maintain good balance on a page, use contrast and proportions effectively and secure a visually attractive publication — cannot be obtained from a computer program. The foundation for these skills needs to be laid elsewhere. If an organisation has its own printing facilities, this lightens the public relations practitioner's burden in that changes, corrections and problems can be attended to quickly. If an outside printer is used, a print job is often more time consuming as copy has to flow back and forth for editing and approval.

The guidelines in this chapter are scaled down to the very basics and are very broad. They focus on general needs arising out of various situations in which public relations practitioners may find themselves. In addition to internal and external house publications, public relations practitioners are often responsible for or involved in, a variety of tasks, including editing articles and taking final decisions on typography, paper, use of photographs, etc.

Basic journalistic skills are adapted to the needs of the public relations practitioner.

What does editing involve?

Editing is the process in which the subeditor (or editor in the case of many in-house journals) checks all the available material in the process of getting everything 'print ready'. This process involves several tasks such as editing copy, pictures and captions. The subeditor is also responsible for writing headlines or editing existing ones for each story. Headline writing is discussed in more detail in chapter 15.

Editing can be done electronically (on computer) or on typed (hard) copy. Let us look at the various editing tasks in more detail.

Copy editing

Copy editing involves two important functions, namely, the editing of content and the editing of language and grammar. At daily newspapers, the responsibility of editing the content of news reports and checking the accuracy of facts and their legality rests with 'night news editors' and 'night editors'. Subeditors are responsible for checking language, grammar, spelling, etc.

When a public relations practitioner is the editor or subeditor of a publication, all these responsibilities lie with him or her.

The public relations practitioner should first read the story to ensure it has value for the publication and its readers. Although articles for such a publication will consist mostly of soft news and human interest stories, they must still be newsworthy — in other words, new, relevant, important or of interest to readers.

Once the public relations practitioner is satisfied an article can be used and the topic is appropriate for the readers and the publication, he or she checks the content for accuracy, ie names, dates, etc. Spelling, grammar and language are also checked and editorial comments are restricted to editorial articles and columns. The public relations practitioner also sees to it that sentences are short and to the point and that copy is written according to the organisation's house style. The story's sequence is also checked.

It is important to keep in mind that, although a subeditor's tasks on any publication are almost the same, style will influence the final product greatly. Articles for house publications differ from newspaper reports and are written in a more relaxed and informal style (rarely with 5W + 1H as points of departure).

Copy editing includes editing the captions of photographs and this should be done with great care. Writing good captions is an art we elaborated on in chapter 15.

When editing on computer, most editing tasks can be completed with little effort. There is no need to make use of the editing symbols needed for hard copy.

If the subeditor uses outside writers, layout artists or printers, he or she often has to work on hard copy using internationally recognised editing signs.

Write in the margin	Description	Example of sign used in the text
⟨ ⊙	Insert full stop	He was here⟨
⟨ '	Insert comma	...witness⟨discover and enjoy.
⟨ '	Insert apostrophe	Mollys second child⟨
⟨ " ⟨ "	Insert quotation marks	⟨I refuse to do it!⟨

EXAMPLE: COPY AS EDITED BY A SUBEDITOR

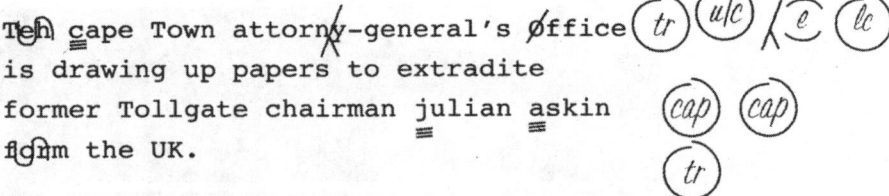

Figure16.1 The most important editing symbols and an example of copy edited in this way (marked copy).

Picture editing

When editing pictures, there are several factors to keep in mind, including the content of the picture, its composition, balance and tone. The picture should be relevant to the story and it should also add balance to the page. The tone or contract should be good enough to be satisfactorily reproduced (Hodgson 1993:62—63).

Although pictures (photographs) are usually edited during layout, this can also be done beforehand. Editing photographs for newspapers is usually left until the layout commences. This is the ideal time to decide which pictures to use and how much space to allocate to them.

When planning a magazine, however, editing photographs beforehand will not only lead to a better final product, but will also enable you to originate more or better photographs.

Cropping

There are two processes involved in picture editing, namely cropping and sizing/scaling. When cropping photographs, any redundant or unnecessary parts are marked on the back with a special marker. As certain markers are not permanent, cropping marks can also be made on the picture itself for removal after it has been used. Cropping a photograph will, to a large extent, determine the focus or focal point. The composition should not be disturbed by cropping and aspects such as space, thirds, background, etc should be kept in mind.

An L-shaped piece of paper acts as a good guide in identifying unwanted parts of a photograph. You can block out sections with the L-shape positioned horizontally or vertically before making a final decision on which part to crop. One leg of the L-shaped template can also be used effectively. The two legs need not always be the same width.

Figure 16.2.A & Figure 16.2B Ways in which an L-shaped template can be used to get rid of wasted space

Sizing/scaling

Once wasted space has been marked, the part of the photograph that will be used can be enlarged or reduced (sized or scaled) to fit an allocated space. This means that a relatively small head-and-shoulders photograph of an important person can be enlarged to almost double its size, depending on its quality. The better the quality of the photograph, the more you can enlarge it.

Before editing a photograph, its purpose in the publication should be clear. Sometimes it merely informs or lends visual appeal to the story. Both instances would apply in the case of a head-and-shoulders photograph of the MD or financial director accompanying an article commenting on a budget. On the other hand, a picture can tell its own story, eg a jubilant, winning sports team. Editing is sometimes essential, eg where the background is unacceptable. A good picture should need no editing.

The process of scaling/reducing a photograph is very simple and can be done in the following way:

▶ *Draw a light diagonal line with a pencil on the back of the photograph.*
▶ *Starting from the bottom corner where the diagonal line begins, measure a horizontal line (at the bottom of the picture) to the new, required width (eg two or three columns).*

- Draw a vertical, dotted line from the new, required width until it intersects the diagonal line.
- Complete the exercise by drawing a horizontal, dotted line from the intersection.

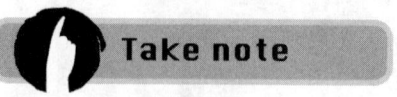

Take note

The same procedure is followed when enlarging/sizing photograph. However, the photograph is then placed at the right, lower corner of a plain piece of paper. The required size can then be marked on the paper.

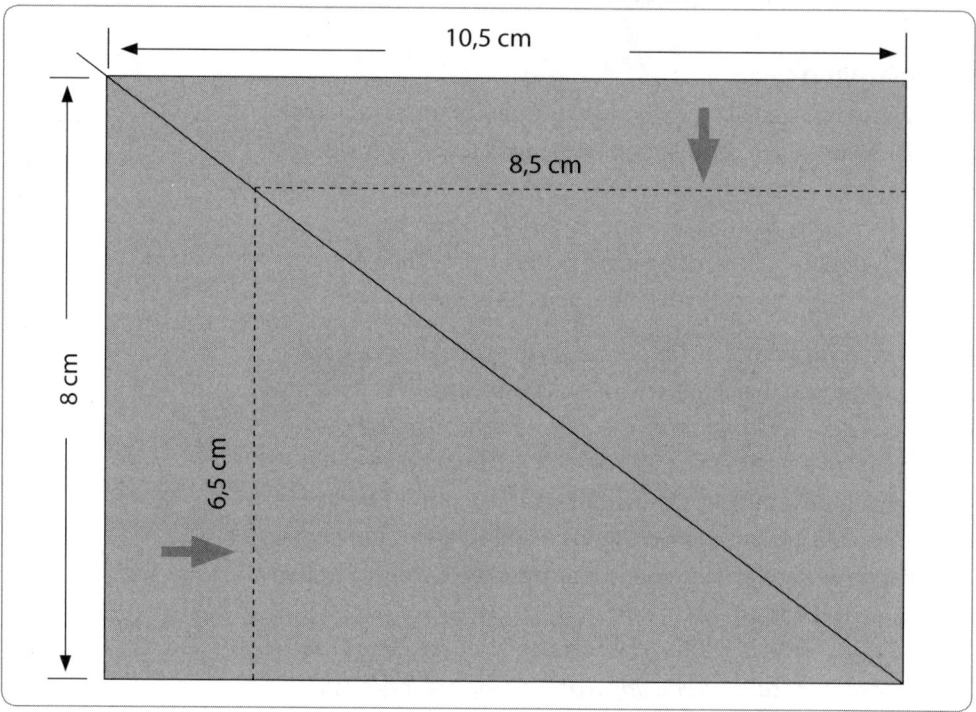

Figure 16.3 Enlarging/sizing a photograph

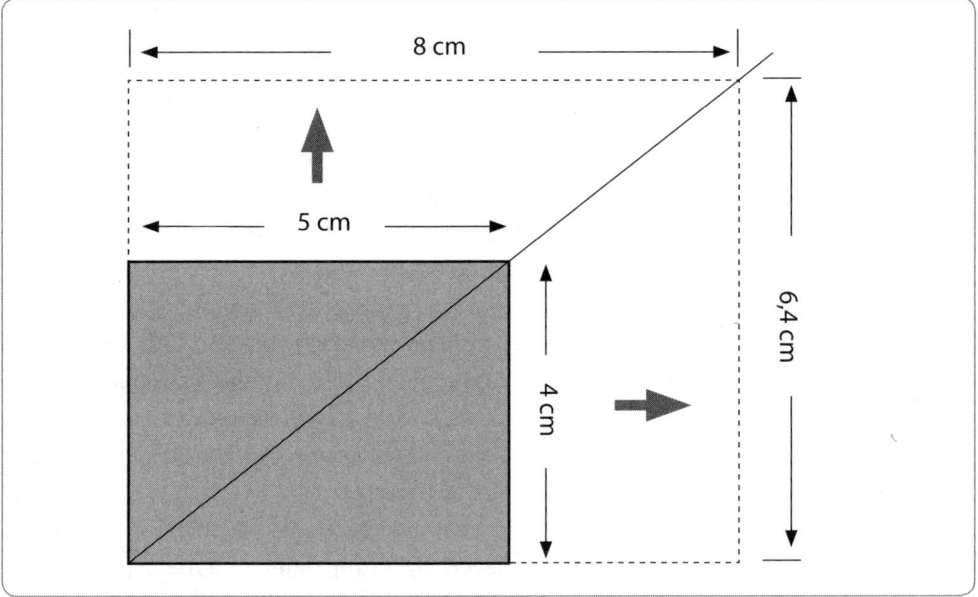

Figure 16.4 Reducing/scaling a photograph

Approaching page layout

Page layout is an art. Although certain guidelines ensure a visually attractive publication, some of these guidelines are sometimes purposefully ignored by layout experts with interesting and positive results. Ignoring them altogether, however, often leads to disaster. The awful consequences become clear only when the publication is printed.

Page layout skills are essential to the public relations practitioner responsible for publications. Although different formats can be used for different publications, the same general principles apply to all of them. Simplicity is the layout artist's watchword — especially when working with smaller publications (in A4 or A5 format).

A basic knowledge of page composition, including aspects such as balance, contrast, proportion, proximity/unity, repetition/consistency and white space, is important to ensure a visually attractive publication. But what do these terms mean?

▶ **Balance** is the arrangement of the various elements on the page. Balance can be used to create a certain mood. For example, to create tension, one may throw elements out of balance.

In order to balance a page, ensure that each portion of the design adds to the balance of the entire page. In practice, this means that balance refers to the way in which headlines, photographs and reports are used in relation to one another and to advertisements. Balance can be maintained in different ways. The traditional or conservative method is to balance the two vertical halves or the two horizontal halves of a page. The more modern approach allows for artistic freedom. Whatever the method, the result should always be a visually attractive publication with a definite focal point. The modern approach can also lead to stunning layouts in which the content and composition of a publication, ie sensational headlines, body copy and pictures are intertwined to stimulate sales. Weekend newspapers, eg the *Sunday Times* and *Rapport*, often use this layout.

▶ **Contrast** occurs when two elements are different. In practice, contrast is achieved by using different typefaces; different sizes of typeface; large and small pictures; bold, medium and 'reversed out' headlines; horizontal and vertical reports; screens; borders; shades of colour; etc. Contrast makes different design elements stand out. The greater the difference of the elements, the greater the contrast. Using bold **type** is one way of creating contrast. Bold can be used to highlight or to emphasise important points. Another way to create contrast is to use different font sizes (larger) with a **bold type** (darker). This will assist in setting headlines apart from the rest of the text. However, remember not to overuse bold. For example, an entire paragraph in bold will make the text difficult to read.

▶ **Proportion** on a page refers to the extent to which body copy can be fitted into interlocking blocks of different sizes, differing in length and width. Newspapers seldom adhere to modular layouts as they become monotonous. Advertisements also preclude their use.

▶ **Proximity/unity** creates a bond between elements on a page. Every page should unify the copy, pictures, headlines and advertisements. The different pages of a newspaper should also form a stylistically coherent whole. To create proximity/unity on a page and to ensure that your page looks organised, you need to space items according to their relation to one another. To create this, ensure that related items appear closer together than items that are not related. The reader will be able to use the spacing as a visual cue and to differentiate what is related and what is not.

▶ **Repetition/consistency** refers to the frequency of using design elements. Consistent use of type and graphics styles and the repeat use of design elements ensure that readers know where to go and to help them to find their way through the designs and layouts. Readers also become more comfortable when certain elements repeat themselves at consistent intervals. In practice, repetition can be created by using the same font for all headlines and the same graphic rule at the top of all pages in a multi-page document and by adding in repeat elements (like page numbers) in the same location on each page.

▶ **White space** refers to the absence of any text or graphics. This ensures that the page does not appear too cramped and also ensures easy reading and less confusion. If a page is too cramped, it becomes difficult to read.

All about typography

Typography plays an important visual role. There are many typefaces to choose from and incorrect choices can detract from a page's visual appeal.

Typography: the style and appearance of printed matter

Typefaces can be divided into two categories: serif and sans serif. Serif characters vary in thickness of stroke and finish with a decorative tail (the serif). Sans serif letters are characterised by even strokes (Hodgson 1993:46).

Typefaces: a set of types or characters in a particular design

Serif	Sans serif
Times New Roman	Helvetica Light
Garamond Bold	*Helvetica Light Italic*
Palatino	**Helvetica Bold**
Century Schoolbook	***Helvetica Bold Italic***
Bookman	Avante Garde

Figure 16.5 Examples of serif and sans serif letters

Serif faces often used by newspapers include Times New Roman, Caslon Bold, Century Bold, Bodoni and Cheltenham. Popular sans serif typefaces include Gill Sans, Metro, Gothic and Helvetica.

Times Roman	*Times Italic*
Times Bold	Helvetica
Helvetica Italic	Optima
Optima Italic	**Optima Bold**
Optima Bold Italic	Helvetica Light
Helvetica Light Italic	**Helvetica Bold**
Helvetica Bold Condensed	Century Schoolbook

Figure 16.6 Examples of typefaces used by newspapers

A popular variation of the serif family, slab serif, differs slightly in that the serifs are squared. An example of slab serif is Rockwell (Hodgson 1993:46–47).

Rockwell

Other typefaces that can be used effectively in public relations are: Old English, Script and Novelty. These typefaces are characterised by their decorative appearance. They are often not very legible and are used mostly for purposes other than text, for example, on invitation cards, etc.

Brush Script

Zapf Chancery

Old English

The different typefaces can also be printed in *italic* (cursive), a sloping of the type to the right from the vertical position.

Times Roman Italic	*Garamond Italic*
Palatino Italic	*Helvetica Italic*

Figure 16.7 Examples of italic fonts

Typefaces can be used in different sizes, with variations in the height, width and weight of letters. All the different characters of one typeface in one size is called a *font*.

Let us look at the height, width and weight of letters.

Height

In addition to the normal height of a letter, the x-height is also important.

Because publications mainly use lowercase type, the height of letters is largely determined by the body height of lowercase letters, referred to as the x-height. The body of a letter excludes the ascenders, eg the upper parts of b, d, etc, and descenders, eg the lower parts of g, y, etc. The vertical measure of the body part (as in 'o' or 'u') is called the x-height.

Figure 16.8 Measuring x-height

Although the x-height of different fonts will not affect the space needed for copy, it creates an optical illusion as seen below:

Figure 16.9 Comparing the x-heights of different fonts

Point size

The size of a letter is determined by the inclusion of both ascenders and descenders, and indicated in point size. Point size can vary from very small, eg 5 point, to very big, eg 72 point. The most popular size for newspaper copy is 10 point for body copy and 12 point for the introductory paragraph. Sizes from 18 point and up are normally used for headlines. A 72-point headline might be used for a lead story.

Examples of point sizes are shown on the following pages.

Type width

Letters can be printed in condensed (narrower), normal or extended/stretched (wider) forms, although the normal format is used most frequently.

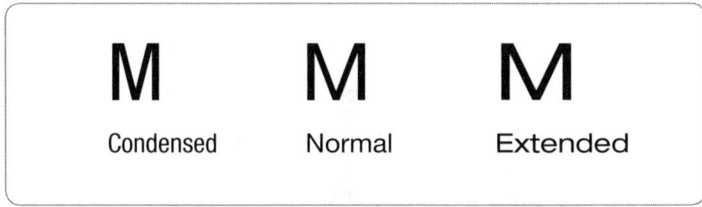

M   M   M

Condensed   Normal   Extended

Figure 16.10 Examples of type width

Type weight

Letters can be set in light, normal and bold types. This refers to the thickness of a letter's lines. Body copy usually has a normal type weight whereas headlines are often set in light and bold for contrast.

There are many options to consider when deciding on fonts and sizes. Consideration would always be given to enhancing the visual appeal of a publication.

Important aspects to bear in mind for layout

If you are an editor, it is your responsibility to ensure that you have enough material to use. Ensure, before deadline, that you have a suitable *lead story* for the front page. If you do not, make sure that you have some interesting stories or a new angle on an existing story, as you might need them unexpectedly.

Lead story: a story given the greatest prominence in a newspaper or magazine

This is 4 point

This is 6 point

This is 8 point

This is 10 point

This is 12 point

This is 14 point

This is 18 point

This is 24 point

This is 30 point

This is 36 point

This is 48 point

This is 60 point

This is 72 point

Figure 16.11 Examples of point sizes

Take note

> *It is important to delegate and manage responsibility in the layout process. When using outside print houses, determine the time they need to complete the job, exactly what they need from you and in what format. It is important not to be too adventurous. Rather play it safe by using familiar methods, choosing known typefaces, sizes, colours, etc.*

A step-by-step guide to page layout

You have now gathered plenty of information and want to compile your publication. What do you do from here? The following steps suggest how the manual layout of a publication can be approached. These steps can be changed to suit different situations and needs:

- ▶ Select articles according to what can be used on which page.
- ▶ Choose a lively, colourful and captivating picture for your front page. Try to use a photograph or graphics on each page to add to its visual appeal.
- ▶ Fitting and sizing headlines form part of layout and must also be done during the layout process.
- ▶ Decide on the content for the front page first as this is the window of the publication and deserves the best material and pictures.
- ▶ Every page should be visually attractive. According to research findings, a reader's eye normally follows a reversed six pattern on a page. Try to fit the lead story of any page on the upper third of the reversed six.

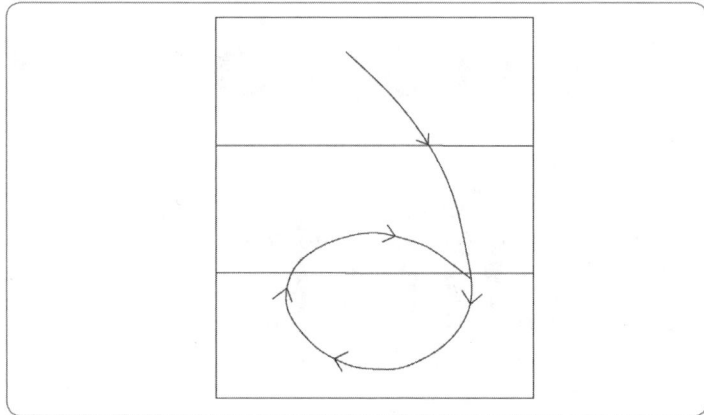

Figure 16.12 The reversed six layout pattern

If you are working to an A3 size, six or seven vertical columns are normally a good guideline to work on. Each column is approximately 39 cm long.

Columns: the vertical, typed copy columns appearing on a page of a newspaper

Figure 16.13 Example of page plan with seven vertical columns

Headlines

Headline writing was discussed in chapter 15. Normally, headlines are written during the subediting process. In this section, we look at the many typefaces, letter sizes and weights that can shape headlines.

The use of different fonts for different purposes and decisions on size, weight, etc can be simplified by keeping templates or examples of the sizes and weights of popular fonts in print. This method is followed by many small community newspapers.

As the space available for a headline may restrict your possibilities and word choice, it is advisable to lay the page out first, allocate space to headlines and then write the headline according to the available space of your page plan. With practice, it becomes fairly easy to estimate the space needed for a headline, eg for the front-page lead story, the back page, etc.

Various ways in which headlines can be arranged in the available space

Let us look at how headlines can be arranged in the space allocated to them. Using a specific method often depends on house style, which usually determines the layout method used throughout the publication.

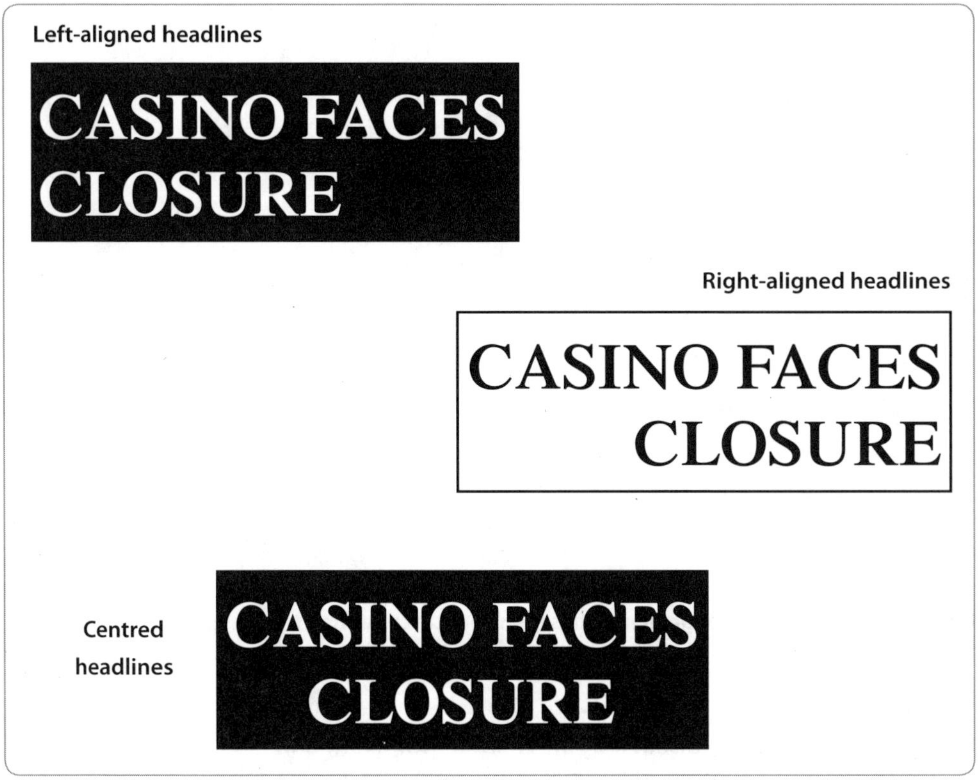

Left-aligned headlines

CASINO FACES CLOSURE

Right-aligned headlines

CASINO FACES CLOSURE

Centred headlines

CASINO FACES CLOSURE

Figure 16.14 Examples of headline alignment

Using subheadings

A heading is often supported by a sub-headline or subheading that can be used above or beneath the headline. This gives more information on the topic.

NEW BUDGET CAUSES CONCERN

MD says he can't support suggestions

or

General feeling of business leaders unchanged

NEW BUDGET CAUSES CONCERN

Figure 16.15 The use of subheadings

How to fit headlines into available space

Headlines can be fitted into the space allocated to them by using the typefaces in the style book and calculating the number of characters for each column.

Writing and fitting headlines is not an easy task and is only brought to perfection through years of experience. At a daily/national newspaper, headlines are normally written by senior staff members with many years of experience.

There is a vast difference between the initial manual way of layout where the typefaces and specific fonts dictated the number of characters that could be used per column. With the change to computer layout, the use of characters is much more flexible. For example, if a headline does not fit properly, various options, such as changing the font or typeface, changing the point (pt) size or stretching/compressing the headline could be exercised until perfection has been reached. Being able to achieve absolute precision and perfectly fitted headlines are some of the advantages of computer layout.

How to mark copy on the page plan

Copy is normally marked in on a page plan according to a set format. Let us assume we have selected the following material for our in-house publication's front page:

> A lead story about a possible merger with another company, plus a photograph of the two managing directors in conversation.
> A photograph of the winner of the recent Comrades Marathon, who holds a senior position in the company, crossing the winning line.
> A sidebar reading 'READ INSIDE'.
> The publication's masthead which runs across the page.

Considering the general rules of layout, we might lay out the page as follows:

> Mark in the *masthead* on the page plan.
> Decide where to place the lead story — remember, the upper third of the page attracts the eye first.
> Allow additional space for headlines.
> Arrange the lead story, photograph and headline so that they form a unit. The lead story must be easily identifiable.
> Mark in the photograph and its caption.
> Mark in the sidebar.
> Make sure that there is no unnecessary 'white space' left over.
> Work on the headlines — decide on the size, fonts, etc.
> Mark in instructions to the printer — circled so that the instructions will not be printed; and
> A blue marker is used for photographs and a red marker for borders.

Masthead: the title of a newspaper placed at the head of; the front or editorial page

On page 215, there is an example of how the above rules might be applied for lay out. Remember, there are several ways in which layout could be done.

Instructions to printers

Instructions on the page plan are important and should be clearly marked. They include the point sizes, borders, upper and lower case, pictures, etc. The marked page plan on page 216 is annotated with instructions to the printers.

Points to remember during layout

▶ Lead stories should be presented as lead stories! This can be done by allocating sufficient space to them and using a large typeface for the headline. A rule of thumb is to use larger headlines for important and long articles and smaller headlines for short and less important stories.

▶ Try to leave as little white space as possible.

▶ Although seven columns per page is a good guideline for an A3 page, they are not mandatory and five or six vertical columns (which will be somewhat wider), can be just as effective. This is especially the case with A4 publications. Any number from two to five columns can be very effective.

▶ If your publication sells advertising space, remember that a specific space is sold at a certain price and that advertisements cannot be moved by the subeditor from the space allocated to it.

▶ Remember to allocate enough space for headlines.

Exercise

You are responsible for the front page of your company's A4 size internal newsletter and decide to use the following material (only draw a rough 'dummy', presuming that this newsletter normally uses three columns per page and that the masthead covers approximately 20% of the page):

▶ *a lead story with a head-and-shoulders photograph; and*
▶ *an action photograph with a caption story.*

Remember that you need to provide space for the masthead, a headline for the story and captions for both photographs.

It is presumed that the text for the lead story is too long and you have to either edit it down to the required length or let the story flow over to another page.

Compare your effort with other existing publications.

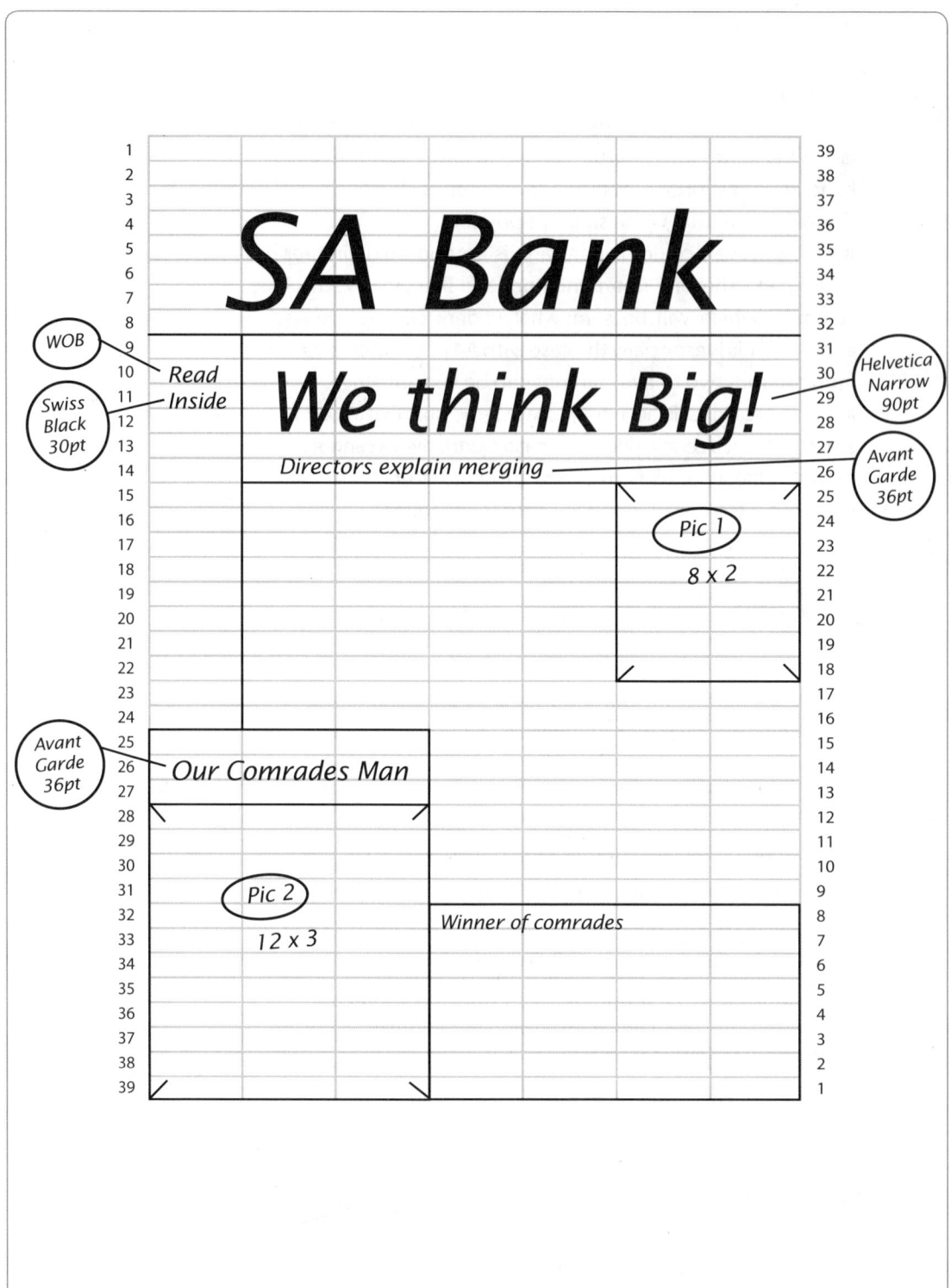

Figure 16.16 Step-by-step instructions on how to layout a particular page using a page plan

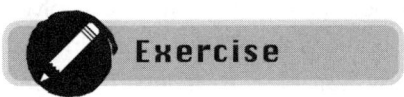

Exercise

You are also responsible for the centre page of this A4 internal publication and decide to create a photo page with photographs taken at the recent 'open day' at your company.

Use two A4 pages, pasted next to each other to create the centre page.

Draw in at least seven to nine picture blocks of different shapes and sizes in a visually attractive manner and write the contents of each picture inside the block. Now write appropriate captions outside the blocks in suitable spaces provided to accompany each picture.

Desktop publishing

Take note

Apart from the equipment, training is an important pre-requisite for DTP. Basic computer skills are not sufficient.

At the beginning of this chapter, we briefly referred to the shift from manual to electronic page layout. We will now take a closer look at what this entails.

Electronic page layout on computer, known as desktop publishing (DTP), is the process of using the computer and specific types of software to combine text and graphics to produce documents such as newsletters, brochures, books, etc. A DTP system allows you to use different typefaces, specify various margins and justifications and insert designs and graphs directly into the text (Desk Top Publishing (dtp) Service Solutions 2010).

DTP is by far the most popular way to do page layout, not only because it results in a professional end product, but also because the right equipment and proper training save much time and effort.

It is important that public relations practitioners who are involved with internal or external publications should first ascertain what computer equipment is already available in their department and to what extent this equipment might be suitable for their specific needs. Smaller programs that might be suitable for a specific task can, for instance, be run on a personal computer (PC), whereas larger DTP programs may need more sophisticated equipment such as an Apple Macintosh computer and/or networks.

Although there is no question about using DTP for regular substantial publications, the viability of electronic layout for any company and the equipment required should be researched thoroughly before any decisions are taken.

Smaller organisations that do not wish to invest in expensive equipment can use the services of an outside layout artist and printer who will do the layout on a DTP program and submit it for approval. This could, however, be time consuming and might not always lead to the end result envisaged.

What is needed for computer layout?

Certain basic equipment is needed for layout on a computer. Firstly, your existing computer has to have sufficient random-access memory (RAM) to operate the program. You also need Windows, (the basic program that accommodates other DTP programs), enough storage space, a colour monitor, a mouse and a printer.

A scanner is also a good option if you often use photographs and have substantial publications. The software package (program) will depend on your specific needs. More sophisticated equipment, such as tools allowing you to draw your own graphics or do finer artistic work, is also available.

In bigger companies who are working on a network, several computers can be used, enabling layout artists to work on different pages at the same time.

Computer companies normally provide excellent advice but always ensure that you clearly spell out your specific needs. There is a vast variety of equipment and software packages on the market and it is no use investing in the most expensive and advanced equipment if you are not going to use it to its optimum. Also remember that training will be a necessity as this is a specialised field.

The team

Electronic page layout is unique in the sense that the end product is much your own creation. A working knowledge of page layout will enable you to create a complete publication from writing articles to finalising the publication and sending it to the printer. The exciting part of electronic layout is that you can use your own creativity in designing each page.

Depending on the size of an organisation, however, there may be a team of people responsible for writing articles and an editor who will decide on a suitable lead story and the contents of each page. The editor will also indicate approximate sizes for stories and photographs. The layout artists, however, design each page allocated to them using the available material according to the style rules of the company.

It is advisable to have more than one person trained to ensure that deadlines are met and that there is always someone available to do the layout. In the case of regular publications, work is often divided between two to three people, each of them responsible for certain pages. It is the editor's job to do the final editing before the pages are sent to the printers.

The process

Much the same guidelines are followed for electronic page layout as described at the beginning of this chapter. Any publication is normally done according to a set of style rules compiled by the specific company or organisation.

Regular internal and external house publications have certain regular articles and columns and have specific spaces allocated to such, ie editor's column, letters, cartoons, etc.

Electronic page layout has the advantage that a set of master pages or templates can be created beforehand and used every time for a specific edition. This means that there will be a ready-made front page, back page, general page, etc that could be used as a basis to work from every time.

Most DTP programs work with picture and text blocks, which means that once you have opened a page on your screen, you first create picture or text blocks on the page and 'import' the pictures or text from the central file server where they have been stored. An article that has been typed on another computer by somebody else and stored on the file server can be called up on the computer of the layout artist and 'imported' into the text block that has been created on his or her page.

The same procedure is followed with photographs, which are scanned in using a scanner and stored on the file server. The layout artist will then create a picture block on his or her page on the screen and 'import' the required photograph.

Once the required text and photographs have been imported, the layout artist must provide space for headlines and type headlines in, different fonts and typefaces may be used for headlines, but most publications prefer only one or two, which they use in different fonts and sizes.

To fit headlines accurately, characters can be vertically or horizontally compressed or stressed or different typefaces can be used. If text and captions will not fit, you can either change the font size or increase/decrease the amount of horizontal or vertical space between items.

Typographic precision can also be obtained by adjusting space between characters or lines, or by resizing the text boxes. Colour, shade and rotating lines as well as text that runs around items and pictures give many exciting options for the final look.

If you are not satisfied with the result, the page can be reduced to only 25% of the screen and the space around the page used as a 'clipboard' where text and photographs can be moved temporarily to provide other options for the layout.

Editing of photographs provides many possibilities. Even bad photographs can be changed to 'good', interesting photographs by making use of some of the following options:

▶ applying colour and shade where necessary;
▶ scaling, cropping, rotating or skewing picture;
▶ changing the standard picture-box shape to another picture-box shape;
▶ applying background colour and shading;
▶ applying frames/borders to picture boxes; and
▶ placing different images in one picture box.

The layout artist should also edit the contents of the text as he or she goes along — especially if there content is too much and should be cut or carried over to a following page.

However, good page layout on the computer only comes with experience. Newcomers in the field should keep the general guidelines of page layout in mind and keep it simple. Ideas on the computer screen may not always turn out so well in the final printed product.

Advantages of DTP

It is obvious from the above discussion that DTP holds many advantages for a professional end result. Once the system is up and running and people are properly trained, the process is also much smoother and faster than outsourcing the work. The list below details a few of the advantages of using DTP:

▶ There is more control over the way text is arranged and formatted.
▶ DTP can be used to bring lots of different files together on the same document.
▶ Do-it-yourself DTP can save money.
▶ It gives you complete control over your final product.
▶ It is easy to make changes.
▶ It provides more ways of communicating ideas effectively.
▶ Images can be imported into a DTP document from a scanner, graphics from a drawing package, frames from a video camera and text from a word processor.
(Desk Top Publishing (dtp) Service Solutions 2010).

The wrong equipment, inadequately trained people and expenses incurred by getting the system in place, however, can result in enormous costs.

 **Summary**

A successful publication lies much in the hands of the public relations practitioner's innovative ideas. To obtain the best results, your layout should be creative and original.

? Test yourself

1. Reduce a photograph, 12 cm wide and 10 cm high, to 8 cm wide.

2. Enlarge a photograph, 4 cm wide and 5 cm high, to 8 cm wide.

3. Describe the difference between copy editing and picture editing.

4. What do you understand by the term 'composition of a page'?

5. Discuss the different typefaces and explain how they differ from one another.

6. Explain type width, weight and height.

7. Discuss the various ways in which headlines can be fitted to the space allocated to them.

8. Discuss the process and use of DTP.

Source consulted

Desk Top Publishing (dtp) Service Solutions (2010) Available at: http://www.articlesbase. com/small-business-articles/desk-top-publishing-dtp-service-solutions-584926.html [Accessed on: 15 August 2010].